OVERVIEW

Overview

How does a company survive for over 100 years? Chances are the answer to that question is never going to be "by doing the same thing it has always done." Typically, corporate survivors have long histories of innovation in both products and business practices. Company history probably includes consolidations, mergers, acquisitions, liquidations, and diversifications, as well as numerous ramp-ups and subsequent layoffs. So the real answer to the question of how a company survives is likely to be "by changing."

For modern companies to survive, even in the short term, change is no longer an option – it's a requirement. In an age where global communication is instantaneous and technological innovations are constant, an organization's ability to change becomes one of its key assets.

Consider how many times things have changed in your work environment in the last few years or even the last few months. How did those changes impact you and your coworkers? Chances are the changes were quite different in each case, with more or less resistance and greater or lesser success. There are different types of organizational change, ranging from incremental improvements to complete overhauls. There are many different methods for dealing with change as well.

This book presents the fundamentals of organizational change, including what is meant by change. The time-honored model of change developed by social psychologist Kurt Lewin in the early part of the twentieth century is used to explain the different phases of change as well as the actions to take in each.

One topic details the two broad categories of organizational change: evolutionary change and transformational change. Within these categories, you'll learn how to distinguish between strategic adjustments, strategic reorientations, and organizational transformations.

Finally, this book covers some of the different theoretical approaches for managing organizational change and the practical application of combining strategies for greater effect.

You'll also learn about weighing the various factors affecting change strategy, such as the time frame and extent of the change, the potential resistance within the organization, and the risks involved.

It's becoming more and more important to know how to effectively implement change, and how to make your organization more readily changeable.

As a leader, you will be required to manage or lead organizational change throughout your career. A good understanding of change fundamentals will serve as a strong foundation from which to craft your change strategies.

Good leaders know that success is directly related to the support of those they're leading. If you're going to lead organizational change, you need to know how to build support for the change.

Organizational change requires people to change – potentially the way they work, think, their habits, routine, and schedule. Faced with change, especially where their livelihood is concerned, people can react negatively; they may get anxious and defensive. Feelings are affected. As a leader, you need to manage your employees' feelings in the best interest of the organizational change.

So how do you gain support in the face of almost certain resistance? Through open and honest communication. Involve your employees in the change by inviting their input, and listening to and considering what they say. Employees are a valuable source of information. And involving them demonstrates you value their opinion and respect their contributions, which will build support for the change.

This book explores tips, techniques, and strategies that will help you successfully build support for change in your organization.

Promoting support for organizational change will require you to motivate, listen, and support your employees through the change.

Motivate

You need to build motivation for change. Do this by demonstrating why the change is a good thing. It's important that employees believe the change will deliver on its promise of improvement and that there's something in it for them.

Listen

To build support for change, you have to listen. Invite employees to provide input on the change. Let the employees know you respect and value their input by actively listening to what they say. Then consider whether their input should be part of the change being implemented.

Support

As a leader, it's your responsibility to support employees through the change. Change can be stressful and scary. It's your job to manage the change in a way that reduces employee anxiety and improves acceptance of the change.

Upon completion of this book, you'll have a set of strategies to use in building support for organizational change.

There's an old adage that says behind the very first person to light a fire, there were two more waiting to stamp it out. What's clear from this simple saying is that if change is inevitable, so too is resistance to that change.

In the modern business world, the success of any technology, innovation, or social advance created by an organization is dependent on how that organization fosters or inhibits change.

Have you ever worked on a change initiative that failed, even though you put in the effort to make sure it was well planned? What do you think caused the change to flounder?

In situations like these, the critical factor is often resistance to change. You may have believed that the path you proposed was the best one to follow, but that doesn't mean your employees perceived it in the same light.

Employees may develop beliefs that the change is not in their best interest or that of the organization. Or they may react emotionally – feeling fear, confusion, apprehension, or skepticism.

When employees react negatively to change, it inevitably leads to some form of resistance. They might actively try to prevent change from happening or being successful. Or they might resist passively by ignoring or eluding involvement in the change.

Dealing with change is a challenge replete with issues to solve and opportunities to utilize. In this book, you'll learn about resistance to change, including the symptoms of resistance, the roots of resistance, and how to manage resistance in your own employees.

During a change process, the emphasis is often on getting the job done now and worrying about everything else later. But when "later" arrives, how will you ensure that you can sustain organizational change, maintain motivation, and keep performance levels up? Even after organizational change is initiated, your work as manager or leader is just beginning. Organizations can't relax; they must constantly improve and keep people motivated toward change.

If you don't remember to also focus on continuing to support the changes you make, all your hard work at the beginning and middle of the process will be lost.

You might be tempted to sit back and relax after change has happened. When a new system, process, structure, or environment is up and running, you could be forgiven for thinking you're at the end of the line.

But the fact is, you're not at the end. You're at the beginning of a new way of working. And when any new way of working is introduced, you have to think about how to sustain and improve performance.

Building a culture that incorporates change into the fabric of the organization requires special effort. Chen, an experienced change manager, has learned from experience that, after change, employees often just want to slip back into old ways of working.

Without a dedicated effort to sustaining change, Chen saw "backsliding" in performance, collaboration, and teamwork. But she pushed forward to keep improving performance, instead of letting things slide.

And by sustaining ongoing improvement, she found new opportunities for employee development and learning. She was able to build on the momentum that results from implementing change.

As Chen discovered in her department, organizational change can be sustained with a little effort. In this book, you'll learn to maintain the momentum of change in a number of ways:

- by creating a collaborative team environment among employees that supports the gains made during change,
- by using the appropriate method of collecting employee feedback regarding change so you can evaluate the change initiative and its effect, and
- by managing and supporting performance after change to ensure productivity, develop

employees, give employees confidence, and avoid conflicts.

After change has made a major transformation in your organization, you need to engage, excite, and support the biggest driver for success in your organization – your people. After all, just because you made improvements a few months ago doesn't mean things will still be working well for you later on. Company goals, leaders, and employees all change frequently. But if you can manage your people as a collaborative team, they'll continue to support and maintain the benefits of change initiatives.

CHAPTER 1 - UNDERSTANDING CHANGE

CHAPTER 1 - Understanding Change
  SECTION 1 - Understanding Organizational Change
  SECTION 2 - Types of Organizational Changes
  SECTION 3 - Approaches to Managing Organizational Change

SECTION 1 - UNDERSTANDING ORGANIZATIONAL CHANGE

SECTION 1 - Understanding Organizational Change

The long-standing model originally put forth by Kurt Lewin describes change as a process of unfreezing from an existing state, transitioning, and then freezing into a new solid state. Unfreezing involves loosening up the current mind-sets and traditions of the organization in order to make possible the transition to the new way of doing things. The traditional view is that, after the transition has been made, the change must then be embedded in the organization during the freeze phase.

But in today's fast-paced business environment, the need for change is constant and the number of changes needed is rapidly accelerating. Organizations must reconsider how they view change and become more readily changeable. Instead of refreezing processes, methods, and values to a solid, enduring state, it may be better to build in a degree of fluidity. Organizations can prepare for upcoming changes by making the next unfreezing phase less difficult.

IMPORTANCE OF ORGANIZATIONAL CHANGE

Importance of organizational change

In business, change is now the rule and not the exception. In the past, well-established industry giants had little to fear from newcomers. But now more than ever before, the top companies are brand new companies. Change – fueled by rapid technological advancement and instantaneous communication – has become a primary factor in business success. And change is getting more rapid all the time. As an organizational leader, you must now be an expert on change to help your company survive and thrive.

Whether you're leading a Six Sigma implementation, helping your company go global, or deploying a new data management system, your change initiatives must be well managed to succeed. But in a rapidly changing world, managing change is not a one-shot deal. It's not a question of finding the one perfect answer to your organization's "problem" and then fixing it for all time.

The traditional approach to change holds that, once achieved, the new way of doing things must be set in stone. In the reality of a fluid business world, however, the emphasis must shift from managing a single change to making organizations changeable.

Organizations must learn to adapt and evolve. Innovations, improvements, and adaptations are all changes that impact a workforce. Consider the example of one global corporation that tried to restructure its Research and Development Department from a traditional top-down hierarchy to a self-managed team-based system. Executives knew their current process was old-fashioned. By implementing an innovative new system, the company hoped to gain a competitive advantage over other firms.

But after what seemed like a well-executed change initiative, the company discovered things weren't going well. Some older research projects could not be aligned with the new way of doing things and glitches in the conferencing software applications produced significant delays in moving projects through the system.

Overtime hours were required and outside contractors were brought in at great expense to make up for shortfalls, and the firm fell even further behind its competitors. After these problems were brought under control, research workers had lost motivation for future change initiatives because of the poor results from the current one.

It became clear to the company's management that the ability to embrace change is a business imperative. In fact, it's a matter of survival for modern businesses. Companies need to be adaptable and flexible to survive in today's markets.

Managing Organizational Change

A structured approach to effectively manage ongoing change needs to be in place for organizations to gain and keep competitive advantage. As a leader, you should continually seek alignment of your organization and the marketplace.

Question

Why is it important to be able to embrace and manage organizational change?

Options:

1. You and your company will be able to effectively introduce innovation and improvements to gain or maintain a competitive advantage
2. You'll know how to achieve the adaptability and the flexibility needed to survive in today's markets
3. Companies that know how to embrace change rather than resist it can reduce costs
4. Learning to manage organizational change will help reduce the number of changes you have to deal with as a leader

Answer

Option 1: This is a correct option. In an ever-changing marketplace, the ability to innovate is vital to getting ahead.

Option 2: This is a correct option. If the market is ever-changing, then the ability to change with it is a valuable tool for survival and success.

Option 3: This is an incorrect option. Embracing change will help a company gain competitive advantage, but not necessarily by reducing costs. Sometimes new processes are more expensive.

Option 4: This is an incorrect option. Change management is not about defending against unwanted changes but rather about being adaptable to changing environmental and market conditions.

ORGANIZATIONAL CHANGE MANAGEMENT

Organizational change management

Organizational change is large scale, companywide change. Smaller changes such as adding a new person or modifying a program don't require the same systematic approach as broader changes that affect diverse groups and entire company cultures. Organization wide changes are things such as a change in mission, a restructuring of operations, or process improvement programs such as Total Quality Management, just-in-time inventory management, or Six Sigma process improvement.

Organization wide change is difficult, and it's no wonder people and organizations sometimes resist it. Change can be costly, annoying, and many times ineffective. Constant change is unsettling. Even those who are aware of the importance of change often fail to focus on making their organizations changeable.

Triggers, initiation, and drivers of change

Change is usually initiated when there is a benefit expected. Change initiatives shouldn't be initiated just for the sake of change.

But no matter what triggers the change, it's normally initiated and translated into action by a person with a vision. Someone perceives benefits such as greater sales, increased efficiency, improved image, or higher employee retention, for example. The vision becomes a plan and the change is put into practice.

After a change plan is translated into action, the scope of an organizational change can often extend to every corner of an organization, including changes to the organizational culture as well.

The organization may face a fundamental realignment of values and mission affecting diverse areas of a company, from IT systems to legal compliance to hiring practices.

In making organization wide change, there may be several barriers and types of resistance to be overcome:
- change goals may conflict with some organizational goals,
- some people won't recognize the need and won't want to change,
- not all people will benefit from the change, and it may even have disadvantages for some of them, and
- changing a way of doing things will require additional effort.

Goals may conflict

A rightsizing change initiative, for example, may conflict with the long-standing goals of an organization that prides itself on stellar customer service, something it may no longer be able to provide.

Some people won't recognize the need

No matter how well you communicate the need for change, some people may refuse to be convinced and resist either actively or passively.

Disadvantages for some people

A quality initiative such as Six Sigma could lead to the downsizing of a quality control department. Inspectors whose jobs will be lost as a result will probably be less than enthusiastic about the change initiative.

Additional effort required

Change may involve more effort in the form of new work procedures, necessary training, and a period of awkward transition as employees learn new procedures.

To overcome these difficulties, it's important to get the people affected to buy in to the change. This can be achieved through effective change management, which involves, among other things, open and frequent two-way communication, incentives, and education about the reasons for the change.

PHASES OF ORGANIZATIONAL CHANGE

Phases of organizational change

As with any journey, change is a process of moving from the current condition to the desired one. In the case of a journey, there's a starting point, the journey itself, and an end. Since the early twentieth century, organizational change has typically been viewed in a similar way using psychologist Kurt Lewin's unfreeze, transition, freeze model. Lewin considered the successful execution of these three phases of organizational change to be the key to getting employees to reach a new mind-set with a new way of doing things.

Unfreeze

The first phase of Lewin's change model involves loosening up or unfreezing the current mind-set and traditional way of doing things. During this phase, the organization gets ready to move from the current state to the new, more desirable one.

Transition

The second phase of Lewin's model is the transition phase, or the change itself. The difference between the unfreezing stage and this stage is the same as the difference between making the decision to travel and taking the first steps.

Freeze

Freezing, or refreezing as some have called it, is the third phase of Lewin's model. This stage is about re-establishing stability once the new way of doing things has been achieved. Freezing involves taking steps to ensure that the new ways of doing things are firmly embedded so that the organization doesn't slip back into a less desirable way of doing things.

Change begins with unfreezing, or overcoming inertia and dismantling the existing mind-set. You can't force change. That would be like getting behind an elephant and trying to push. No matter how hard you try, the elephant isn't going to move until it wants to. Unfreezing involves creating a case for change by convincing the organization that the problem exists and is urgently in need of a fix. Only then can you begin to sell a particular solution.

If the existing structure is not first loosened up, you will encounter strong resistance to the change. You can loosen the structure by articulating a clear and compelling vision that describes what the change effort is striving to accomplish.

Use whatever persuasion skills you have to persuade yourself and others of the need for change. Let others know the problem exists and that it needs addressing urgently.

Financial or sales data relative to your competitors can be useful to help unfreeze employee mind-sets. Lewin developed a tool that is particularly useful for the unfreeze phase of change called force field analysis.

Applicable to a number of disciplines, this approach deals with the factors driving movement toward change and those that hinder change. Force field analysis is simply an organized method to weigh up the pros and cons of a situation. If the pros outweigh the cons, people will be motivated to change.

After employees' attitudes are unfrozen, change begins to happen. This is the second phase of organizational change – the transition phase. Once people are mentally prepared to change, they must take the necessary steps and make the changes. This is a period of uncertainty as old ways are challenged and changed, but the new methods have yet to prove themselves. Providing support for the change is vital at this stage.

Training and resources

Support can take the form of training, coaching, and providing resources. Role models are also valuable for supporting the change.

Good communication

Good communication is important throughout this period to make sure people have a clear idea of what's expected of them and to continually reinforce the benefits of completing the change.

Expect mistakes

It's important to communicate that mistakes are expected, and even welcomed, as part of the learning curve. Encourage people to be hands-on and develop their own solutions.

There are many other recommended activities and tips for the transition phase:

set up small achievable steps to make the overall change less overwhelming and help build momentum

give everyone a role to play in the implementation process

encourage people to give suggestions and feedback

continue providing strong, clear communication about the need for the change and status of the change

take time to reflect on how things are going, make adjustments, and remember to celebrate milestones, and

enforce new policies and procedures to ensure people don't revert to their old ways

As the transition phase moves in to the freeze phase, changes are embedded. This final phase of Lewin's model is often called refreezing because it's where the organization returns to a stable state with the new goals, values, or methods solidly in place. It can take time and effort for change to be locked in and for people to reach a new comfort zone.

In the freeze phase, many of the same means of effective change management must continue, including strong, clear, ongoing communication and support.

In addition, old methods, procedures, and resources should be removed, so that there's no turning back. Formalize the change by documenting the new company standards, policies, and practices.

Align reward systems with the new way of doing things. Make a break from rewarding the old values to avoid confusion.

Consider the case of a candy manufacturing company that was instituting a new companywide defect tracking system. The need for the new system was communicated repeatedly to employees during the unfreeze phase. During the initial presentation for the change initiative, customer satisfaction data was presented that showed the urgent need to become more quality minded to retain market share.

During the transition phase, employees were provided with ample training and assigned a personal coach who would help them with the new tracking methods if they became confused. Benefits of the new program were communicated as they began to accrue and milestones in the change process were celebrated at monthly meetings.

In the freeze stage, employees were asked to locate and destroy any legacy documentation from the previous tracking system. Successes and milestones continued to be highlighted and celebrated.

The freezing phase might seem to be the end of the journey but in light of our fast changing world, it should be considered a new starting point instead. Freezing should include reinforcing the change to avoid things slipping backwards and to ensure the changes remain in place as long as needed. But to aim for too "solid" a freeze of the new ways may be counterproductive. The organization should remain somewhat flexible so that unfreezing is easier the next time things need to change.

Question

You're leading a production change initiative at a manufacturing company. The company has a traditional culture and mind-set, and the department heads are reluctant to change methods they believe are working.

Match the phases in the change process to the corresponding actions you can take to facilitate change.

Managing Organizational Change

Options:
A. Unfreeze
B. Transition
C. Freeze

Targets:
1. Highlight the forces for and against the change to persuade department heads to get on board
2. Provide well-trained coaches for each project team to ensure understanding of the new production methods
3. Replace all old manuals and procedural instructions with new materials

Answer

Highlighting the forces for and against the change – as in a force field analysis – is an example of the type of activity undertaken during the unfreeze stage. The activity helps employees become ready and willing to take the first step.

Coaching and mentoring employees is an activity associated with the transition phase, or the change itself. As workers face unfamiliar methods and unproven results, they need support.

Removing old materials to ensure employees don't refer to old methods is an activity associated with the freezing phase. It helps ensure problems are dealt with using the new methods.

SECTION 2 - TYPES OF ORGANIZATIONAL CHANGES

SECTION 2 - Types of Organizational Changes

Organizational changes fall into two broad categories: evolutionary and transformational. As the name implies, evolutionary change, which can take the form of strategic adjustments or strategic reorientation, is incremental change that occurs over time.

Transformational change involves a fundamental reevaluation and redirection of the core business of an organization. It's less common, and frequently unsuccessful. This is all the more reason why, as a leader, you should know how to identify which type of change you're dealing with and apply the appropriate techniques to implement it.

TYPES OF CHANGE

Types of change
"Here today, gone tomorrow." That isn't the most comforting thought to stakeholders. But even in a rapidly changing business world, companies can change their motto to "Here today, still here tomorrow" by becoming less rigid and more changeable. No one can predict whether the current trend of rapid change will continue or whether it will increase even further. But given the strategic importance of change, adaptability and flexibility will continue to be a source of competitive advantage.

Organizational leaders must be able to recognize the different types of change if they are to embrace change and adapt. The two broad categories of change are evolutionary change and transformational change.

Evolutionary change enhances the current way of doing things by employing new technology, policies, or procedures. This is the most common type of change. With evolutionary change, certain parts of an organization are altered over time.

Sorin Dumitrascu

Transformational change is less common because it involves a fundamental shift in the way an organization does things. It may require changes to operations, customers, or even the values an organization holds dear.

EVOLUTIONARY CHANGE

Evolutionary change

Most changes are evolutionary and alter existing models or systems over time. They come from interacting with customers or vendors, from improvement and innovations in processes, or in reaction to environmental or market forces. Even the best laid plans can't predict how an organization will perform once it hits the real world. As problems are encountered, evolutionary changes in the form of strategic adjustments or larger scale strategic reorientations are needed.

Strategic adjustments represent the fine-tuning of processes. While these day-to-day, incremental changes may lead to a new strategic direction, they don't begin with an overarching strategy other than improvement and adjustment.

Strategic adjustments are made to address situations as they arise and are primarily aimed at achieving short-term gains. These are the changes every business makes to attract and retain customers, improve products and processes, and meet changing regulatory and market requirements.

Adjustments are the constant and natural changes that happen as an organization grows and develops. They involve minor improvements to the system as it exists and, as such, require managerial skill more than leadership ability. The evolutionary changes made by a certain coffee shop chain offer examples of strategic adjustments.

Environment

The price of the primary coffee used in the company's famous house blend has skyrocketed due to political instability in the region where it's produced. To respond to this environmental change, the company introduces and heavily promotes a new house blend, which uses a less expensive coffee as its foundation. By shifting attention to the new blend, the earlier product can be quietly phased out.

Complaints

Customer complaints about the thinness of the to-go cups led the company to start using a thicker, more environmentally friendly cup from a different manufacturer for the same price.

Competitors

In response to their competitor's new discount card program, the shop instituted a members club card offering significant discounts to repeat customers.

Strategic reorientation – the other type of evolutionary change – involves a change in strategy, either through adjusting elements of an existing one or by adopting a new strategy. Unlike strategic adjustments, which are modifications of operations that may in the long run affect strategy, strategic reorientation begins at the strategic level with a plan to address some significant change in the environment. For this reason, it requires skilled leadership at the organizational level in addition to capable management.

With strategic reorientations, the company's overall strategy remains relatively stable, but the organizational design undergoes some substantial revision. For example, reorientation might involve the introduction of a different type of product to existing customers. Or it might involve introducing the current products to an entirely new market.

A case of strategic reorientation

One familiar strategic reorientation was the marketing of baking soda as a key ingredient of cleansers and air fresheners. In this case, a company took its existing product – baking soda – and introduced it to an entirely new market, while maintaining existing culinary customers. This represented a change in strategy but didn't disrupt or destabilize the company.

Consider the case of a small musical instrument shop that used to make most of its money selling instruments and amplifiers to new music students. With the rise of online marketplaces, instrument sales in the store plummeted as the younger generation in particular chose to purchase through online auctions. Buying used instruments online carried some risks for consumers, however. Instruments often arrived broken, had missing parts, or were in need of adjustment.

In light of this change in the marketplace, the music store shifted its focus from sales to repairs. The owner hired new staff, refocused the store's marketing, expanded repair facilities, purchased new equipment, and re-examined and revised price structures.

This strategic reorientation required the company's employees to develop new skills and knowledge. The effort paid off because, despite declining instrument sales, the store has continued to thrive. No amount of minor adjustments would have allowed the store to reorient itself in time to stay in business. A longer-term solution was needed and provided at a strategic level.

Question

An outdoor equipment company has added new products in response to marketplace changes caused by new technology. Traditionally focused on backpacks, tents, and camp stoves, the firm now sells camouflage cell phones, portable deep fryers, solar rechargers, and a variety of other hi-tech products requiring competencies far afield from traditional camping and hunting expertise.

How would you characterize this type of change?

Options:

1. Strategic adjustment
2. Strategic reorientation

Answer

Option 1: This option is incorrect. The changes made are not simply strategic adjustments because they require new expertise of the company's employees and go beyond small, short-term day-to-day realignment. Moving into new sales areas reflects a leadership decision to shift organizational strategy to some degree.

Option 2: This is the correct option. Branching out to entirely new and different hi-tech products reflects a strategic reorientation. Company executives made the leadership decision to expand the company's offerings into fields requiring new knowledge and competencies. The decision was made at a strategic level rather than an operational one.

TRANSFORMATIONAL CHANGE

Transformational change

Mergers, acquisitions, downsizing, or major marketplace or societal events can prompt the other broad category of change – transformational change. Unlike evolutionary change, this is of a larger scale, involving alteration of a company's core business model. It requires new knowledge, competencies, and abilities as people deal with new products, services, and customers. Although less common than evolutionary changes, more and more organizations are having to face transformational changes to survive.

Fast food restaurants have typically ranked among the top grossing food franchises. As social and economic trends changed in recent years, the dining public became more health conscious. Customers wanted full sit-down meals that offered at least the appearance of quality and a healthier "dining" experience. To compete with the casual dining restaurant chains that were thriving in this period, many fast food restaurants made major strategic shifts, reinventing themselves as places where people could eat well for less money.

Many fast food restaurants embraced a transformational change.

Products

Some fast food chains began to offer specialty coffee, gourmet burgers, steamed vegetables, and relatively exotic salads to attract more discerning customers.

Equipment

Some of the changes in product required retooling. One chain had to install new broilers in all of its restaurants to handle new products, such as char-broiled Angus beef hamburgers.

Marketing

The fast food chains used marketing techniques to present themselves as places where you could purchase a high-quality meal at a bargain price. Quality and healthfulness had previously not resided at the core of their marketing.

Transformational change occurs relatively infrequently. It succeeds infrequently as well. But in the case of the fast food chains, the market turned around and they reclaimed their previous standing.

Unlike strategic reorientations, during which an organization's strategy can remain relatively stable while operations undergo substantial revision, transformational change presents a greater risk.

Transformation requires a fundamental shift in the company mind-set, changes company culture, affects reporting relationships, and realigns responsibilities. Leaders are required to examine and question the organization's core values, vision, mission, goals, strategies, and processes.

In transformational change, the scope is such that the company often risks confusing its existing customers. The need to execute a strategic transformation is relatively rare and that's fortunate because it can be difficult for a company to make such a large shift quickly enough to succeed.

Consider the case of a major petroleum company that has begun shifting its focus to producing solar energy. Executives in the company recognize the eventual change that will hit their industry when petroleum supplies begin to run out and so they're reinventing themselves as an alternative energy provider.

The transformed company will try to appeal to new and different customers, and its employees will need to be knowledgeable in entirely different areas. But as the company is a relatively late entrant into the solar energy field, it's questionable as to whether it can make the transformation in time to succeed.

Question

As a change leader, it's important to be able to recognize the type of change you're dealing with.

Match the types of change to examples of each. A change type may match to more than one example.

Options:

A. Evolutionary change
B. Transformational change

Targets:

1. A company introduces a radically different type of product to its existing market

2. An automobile manufacturer known for producing expensive, gas-guzzling SUVs switches to making small, energy-efficient electric-hybrid cars

3. A company makes its processes become more cost-efficient over time because of innovative improvements to the system discovered during each major project

Answer

When you introduce customers to a radically new product, it's a strategic reorientation and therefore a type of evolutionary change. While somewhat risky, your customer base can continue to provide stability while you alter your strategic approach in a single area.

Completely altering what you produce and who your target customer is, as this auto manufacturer did, is a transformational change. The change is so extensive that there is no stabilizing factor to ensure it remains in business while completing the change.

Incremental improvements, even highly innovative ones, are strategic adjustments. They represent a type of evolutionary change that carries little risk and does not disrupt the business's stability.

SECTION 3 - APPROACHES TO MANAGING ORGANIZATIONAL CHANGE

SECTION 3 - Approaches to Managing Organizational Change

There are many theoretical approaches to managing change. Four that have been identified by experts are empirical-rational, normative - reeducative, power-coercive and environmental-adaptive. Depending on factors such as time frame, benefits, degree of change, resistance, and the overall stakes, some approaches will work better than others as the primary approach for a given situation.

In reality, successful change management usually involves a mix of strategies to address the various aspects of the change. Knowing how to weigh the various selection factors and decide which approaches can be combined is a skill central to effective change management.

CHANGE MANAGEMENT FACTORS

Change management factors

There are many types of change, and new change initiatives are undertaken every day. Each has its own characteristics, objectives, and activities, and may be aimed at fixing anything from customer service, workflow, and employee retention to environmental sustainability. Organizations themselves also differ in size, structure, and culture. Within each organization, different areas have different issues, perform different activities, and fulfill different needs. Naturally, no single approach to change is right for every situation.

You can take a wide variety of approaches to managing change. Before deciding which approach is best suited for a particular situation, you need to examine a number of key selection factors:
- the time frame for the change,
- the extent of the change,
- the amount of resistance to change, and
- what's truly important and at stake.

EMPIRICAL-RATIONAL

Empirical-rational

Experts describe a number of change management approaches you can use to address the variety of situations that can arise. Depending on the selection factors previously mentioned and the culture of the organization, you will likely want to use one of four principle approaches: empirical-rational, normative-reeducative, power-coercive, or environmental-adaptive. Real-life situations usually call for a mix of these theoretical approaches, rather than the use of a single one.

The first approach, described by change experts Bennis, Benne, and Chin, is the empirical-rational approach. This approach to change is built on the assumption that people are basically reasonable.

When you approach change from an empirical-rational point of view, you start with the basic tenet that people do what they think is good for them. Through communication, persuasion, and incentives, you hope to convince stakeholders over time of the need for change. If you do these things effectively, you expect to get buy-in.

So you use an empirical-rational approach when the pros of a situation can clearly be presented as outweighing the cons. Potential rewards must also outweigh the risks, so this approach works best when there is little-to-no risk involved or when staying the same carries more risk or is uncomfortable. If the status quo seems good to employees, they are unlikely to be motivated to change regardless of potential rewards.

On the other hand, if the potential rewards are great, the risks small, and the current situation untenable, reason may very well prevail and people will move toward change. Several strategies are appropriate to an empirical-rational approach:

- One way to spread the word about the benefits of the new program is to take some of the people you first convinced of the benefits and use these early converts to help enlist others.
- Depending on the situation, another tactic for motivating people to accept the change is to focus on the negative aspects of the current state.
- A legitimate tactic for moving people toward the change is to offer them incentives for aligning themselves with the new way of doing things.

The assumption that people are for the most part reasonable and can be persuaded to act in their own self-interest may seem naive to some. But when the upside outweighs the downside of making the change, given time, reason often prevails. Of course, persuading stakeholders is easiest when there is little resistance to the change to begin with and little risk involved.

Question

Do you think the empirical-rational approach can be used successfully when the potential risks of making a change outweigh the benefits?

Options:

1. Yes
2. No

Answer

The most challenging requirement of this approach is that the upside must honestly outweigh the downside of making the change. If the potential risks outweigh the benefits, reason will work against the change and you won't get buy-in.

NORMATIVE-REEDUCATIVE

Normative - reeducative

The second approach identified by Bennis, Benne, and Chin is called normative - reeducative. This approach is more socially and culturally focused. It assumes that since humans are social animals, the primary factor influencing people's behavior is a desire to conform to group values and norms.

Instead of pushing the benefits of a change, normative - reeducative strategies focus on encouraging commitment and conformity to the new way of working. Why? Because, quite simply, everybody else is doing it.

Reeducation is the focus of this kind of "get with the program" approach. You encourage people to adapt to changes as a way to conform to the new norms. Any long-term change strategy must have some normative - reeducative or culturally focused actions involved.

But the normative - reeducative approach presents a few challenges. Before you can get people to go with the flow, you first have to make the new way of doing things become "the flow." And that's not easy. Defining the flow means establishing the new program as the new cultural direction that employees must get on board with. And achieving cultural change is a slow process.

So the normative - reeducative approach works best when you're working with deadlines that are loose rather than tight.

The informal side of an organization can be just as important or more important than the formal organization itself in affecting cultural change. For this approach to be an option, the two have to be reasonably well aligned.

Also, for this approach to work, resistance has to be low. If there is much disharmony or resistance, the new way of doing things will not be perceived as the new "flow" that people need to align themselves with.

Normative - reeducative strategies focus on ways to alter company culture:
- Organizational leaders in positions of power can sway large groups. Charismatic leaders are particularly valuable in helping to institute cultural change.
- In a situation where informal leaders hold as much or more sway as formal ones, it can be good strategy to involve them in reeducating stakeholders.
- Although insufficient in themselves, internal advertising and promotion can help foster cultural change.

POWER-COERCIVE

Power-coercive

Bennis, Benne, and Chin identified a third change management approach they call power-coercive. This approach is based on the assumption that people expect those in charge to tell them what to do and will be inclined to simply do what they are told.

Ways to apply the power-coercive approach

This approach can range from the quiet application of absolute authority to an unsubtle open display of power, as in "Do it...or else."

Either way, employees are given no real options and are expected to comply or face sanctions.

Your situation may have been one of tight deadlines or an immediate threat to the organization. In these cases, the power-coercive approach may be the only viable choice to exert authority over employees in hopes that they get in line.

The use of authority combined with the imposition of sanctions for failing to change may allow you to make changes when the stakes are high or when the initiative faces strong resistance.

If you choose a power-coercive approach, you must consider several factors:
- The modern workforce doesn't necessarily jump when the boss says to jump. Many businesses foster a cultural climate of independent work, autonomy, and entrepreneurship.
- When the situation is – or can be presented as – one of a high level of danger, people will quickly accept authority that they might otherwise balk at.
- When the risks are great, the time frame is short, and people are discontented, a power coercive strategy is more likely to succeed.

Cultural climate

People accustomed to modern autonomous cultural climates won't simply take orders. They will feel their autonomy is threatened and may become even more resistant.

Level of danger

If the situation is such that danger is imminent and people are confused or lack clear direction, they may welcome the reduced options and clear guidance of this approach. Otherwise they may resist.

Risks and urgency

When there is no crisis, no urgency, and people are content, they will tend to resent and resist authoritarian moves.

ENVIRONMENTAL-ADAPTIVE

Environmental-adaptive

Fred Nickols, another change management expert, defines a fourth change management approach he calls environmental-adaptive.

The premise of this approach is that people adjust quickly to change. So in some cases, it may be easier to create a new organization and let the old one die, rather than expend the effort to try to change the existing one.

While this approach bears some resemblance to the power-coercive approach in it's "take it or leave it" philosophy, the difference is that environmental-adaptive methods put the burden on employees. Whoever doesn't adapt is out.

The environmental-adaptive approach aligns best to transformational change. With a large change or a particularly radical change where there's likely to be major resistance, "letting the chips fall where they may" may be the best option. If the new organization won't resemble the previous one very much, then it may simply be easier to skip over resistance to change and concentrate on dealing with the fallout after the fact.

When choosing this approach over others, you want to move people to the new way of doing things and let the old organization die out. That way, people will be forced to adapt to the new way of doing things.

Reaching a certain critical mass of "new" people is vital for this to happen. The new organization must have a sufficient number of converts so that, as everyone transitions, the old types of people don't influence the new culture to revert to the old one.

One strategy to help reach this point is to seed the transformed organization with "new" people – either enthusiastic workers from within the current organization or outside hires familiar with the new ways. Keep in mind, it's not crucial to convert every single person. A few people can sometimes be left behind if they are never going to fit in.

Question

Match each change management approach to the conditions under which it works best. More than one approach may apply to each condition.

Options:

A. Power-coercive
B. Normative - reeducative
C. Environmental-adaptive
D. Empirical-rational

Targets:

1. Low resistance to change
2. Loose deadlines
3. High risk
4. Radical change

Answer

Both the empirical-rational and normative - reeducative approaches work with weak resistance and are often used in combination.

Empirical-rational and normative - reeducative both apply when deadlines are loose. Under those circumstances, you have time to appeal to people's rationality and work for eventual cultural change.

The power-coercive approach suits high-risk or urgent situations. People often welcome the use of authority to make a quick change in a crisis.

The environmental-adaptive approach can be used with really big changes. It avoids wasted effort on promoting change by placing the burden on individuals to adapt.

COMBINING APPROACHES TO MANAGE CHANGE

Combining approaches to manage change

Approaches are just that, ways to come at a problem – in this case, change. With the wide variety of goals, activities, interest groups, and interactions in an organization, a single approach is unlikely to achieve change as effectively as a combination of approaches. Although a particular change initiative may lean in one direction – say, power-coercive – there are likely to be elements of other approaches needed as well.

Question

Before learning to combine approaches, you should be sure you're familiar with their basic premises.

Demonstrate your knowledge of the basic assumptions of the four approaches by matching each approach to its assumption.

Options:

A. Empirical-rational
B. Normative - reeducative
C. Power-coercive

D. Environmental-adaptive
Targets:
1. People do what they think is good for them
2. People want to go with the flow
3. People will do what they are told
4. People will quickly adjust to change

Answer

The empirical-rational approach trusts people to be rational and act in their own best interest.

The normative - reeducative approach has a cultural focus that assumes people want to conform with norms and go with the flow.

The power-coercive approach assumes people expect someone to direct them, and typically they will comply.

An environmental-adaptive approach is based on the notion that people adapt quickly to new situations, so why not leave it to them to adjust.

In one example of combining approaches, a shoe manufacturing company introduced new methods to streamline production, including new workflow, new tracking methods, and new equipment.

The initiative, dubbed the Flow-Fix initiative, was a reaction to a recent market shift and strong overseas competition. Executives believed that to remain competitive in the long run, they needed to constantly improve their production speed.

Resistance to the change was likely to be low as people were dissatisfied with the current state of things. And they were in favor of the company being more efficient and competitive. In the long run, that would make their jobs secure. The plan was to make the transition over several years.

The transition team members considered a number of factors. They noted that the change had distinct benefits and that it would take place over a long period of time. Team members decided the primary approach to use in this case would be empirical-rational. Considering that resistance to the change was likely to be low, team members felt they could "sell" the benefits of the change over time through an internal communication campaign.

But there were also normative-reeducative elements to the change plan the team developed. For example, team members included an incentives program that rewarded those who excelled at the new standards.

Incentives supported the overall empirical-rational strategy by rewarding those who enthusiastically got on board. Instead of focusing on the benefits of the change itself, the normative-reeducative strategy encouraged adherence to the new standards as a way to be compliant.

The two change management approaches were used in combination because both work under the same conditions – when resistance is low and time frames are not tight. Power-coercive strategies and environmental-adaptive strategies were avoided because the change was neither radical nor urgent in this case.

Consider the case of another company – a major accounting firm changing from their traditional central office-based system to a regional team-based system. The company plans to use virtual teams around the world and incorporate work-from-home programs in hopes of lowering costs and providing more attractive working conditions. But the firm is by nature a highly bureaucratic company and most employees have been working for the company for a long time. As a result, the staff members are set in their ways.

Question

There is likely to be considerable resistance to change at the accounting firm. And with the recent trends in the industry, the time frame for making the change is somewhat tight.

Which approaches should executives use to manage the change in this case?

Options:

1. Use an internal promotional campaign to emphasize the cost savings to the company and the increased employee satisfaction that will come from being allowed to work from home

2. Institute sanctions for those who fail to respect the culture diversity in the new company and adopt the new courtesy policies

3. Assign workers to virtual teams and let team leaders work out the details and make adjustments 4. Try to get informal leaders to buy in to the change and get their friends on board

Answer

Option 1: This is a correct option. The empirical-rational approach is useful in this case. The clear benefits of the change that executives can promote to stakeholders – such as cost savings to the company and increased employee satisfaction – will persuade many to embrace the change.

Option 2: This is a correct option. The power-coercive approach can be used in this case with the empirical-rational approach as a supporting strategy. The time frame for this change is relatively tight, so to speed up compliance, executives must exert a little authority.

Option 3: This is an incorrect option. Instituting the change and then letting stakeholders adjust is an environmental-adaptive strategy. It might be effective in a more radical change but no fundamental redefining of the company is happening here. Company values and the work will both remain the same.

Option 4: This is an incorrect option. Although normative-reeducative strategies are useful for long- range plans, the relative urgency in this case calls for more immediate action. There isn't time to try to alter the corporate culture before reorganizing.

Time frame is a significant factor for the accounting company, so the primary approach will be power-coercive. Executives will need to use their authority to get the job done quickly.

But when there are specific benefits, such as better working conditions and cost savings, empirical- rational strategies can act as a supporting secondary approach. Appealing to people's rationality by
highlighting the benefits may help reduce resistance to change.

A normative-reeducative approach is not an option because time is tight and cultural change takes too long. Promoting the benefits is more effective than attempting cultural change to reduce resistance in the short term.

The bureaucratic nature of the organization also argues for the use of power-coercive strategies. Employees are probably used to accepting direction. So being authoritarian will create less resentment than it would in a more autonomous and entrepreneurial work culture such as the one the organization is trying to transition to.

Ginnie is the leader of the transition team at the pharmaceutical company where she works. Her company has just merged with a similar overseas company, a firm that was formerly the company's bitter competitor. Ginnie's strategy illustrates another possible combination of approaches.

Ginnie's organization is undergoing major changes. The merged company will have an entirely new look and will be bilingual, as English is the main language at her old firm and French is predominant at the other firm. All advertising, logos, and promotional literature will be changed.

The new company will even have a slightly different orientation, focusing on natural vitamin supplements in addition to its current line of health-related products. For these reasons, Ginnie has decided that her team will use a combination of the environmental-adaptive and power-coercive approaches.

Environmental-adaptive

The change Ginnie's company is facing is transformational. Workers will hardly recognize the new company. Considering that, and the fact that the partner company was formerly a bitter rival from another culture, the situation has the potential for high resistance. So Ginnie decides that gradually moving from the old organization to the new one would never work. She will primarily employ an environmental-adaptive strategy.

Power-coercive

Ginnie's team ensures that stakeholders are all made aware of the reasons for the change and how important it is for the company's survival that the merger happen quickly. This message helps ease the pain of the power-coercive supporting strategies that Ginnie must use to ensure a successful transformation. Employees found violating new procedures repeatedly are quickly removed or demoted. Any uncooperative or culturally insensitive behaviors are swiftly dealt with.

Combining the environmental-adaptive and power-coercive approaches works well when there is a large amount of resistance to change. The empirical-rational and normative - reeducative strategies were ruled out in this case because of the radical nature of the change, the high resistance, and the urgency of the transition.

Question

Which statements about combining approaches to change management are correct?

Options:

1. Empirical-rational and normative - reeducative approaches can be used together when time frames are loose, there's a clear benefit to the change, and a low level of resistance is expected 2. Power-coercive strategies may be used to deal with resistance to an environmental-adaptive approach in the case of a large-scale transformational change where resistance is likely to be high

3. Power-coercive strategies can be used to support a normative - reeducative approach when there are clear benefits to eventual cultural change and a high level of resistance

4. An environmental-adaptive approach can be combined with a normative - reeducative approach by

creating a new culture and simply leaving employees to adapt to it

Answer

Option 1: This is a correct option. An empirical-rational approach, such as pointing out the benefits of a change through advertising and promotion, can be combined with long-term efforts at cultural change. When resistance is low, and change can happen incrementally, both approaches may apply. A normative - reeducative strategy such as enlisting the help of informal leaders can support a primarily empirical-rational approach.

Option 2: This is a correct option. Both the power-coercive and environmental-adaptive approaches work well when resistance is great. Sanctions for incorrect behavior could be used in some aspects of a transformational change to ensure overall acceptance while people adjust to the new way of doing things.

Option 3: This is an incorrect option. The normative - reeducative and power-coercive approaches are not compatible in this case. Normative - reeducative strategies don't work well with high resistance and power-coercive strategies don't work when change is incremental and long term.

Option 4: This is an incorrect option. Environmental-adaptive approaches can be used to make employees adapt to new structures, designs, processes, and systems, but cultural change must happen gradually.

CHAPTER 2 - BUILDING POSITIVE SUPPORT FOR CHANGE

CHAPTER 2 - Building Positive Support for Change
  SECTION 1 - Building Motivation for Change
  SECTION 2 - Listening to Employees during Change
  SECTION 3 - Supporting Individuals through Change

SECTION 1 - BUILDING MOTIVATION FOR CHANGE

SECTION 1 - Building Motivation for Change

All employees, even you, will react to the changes that take place in their organization. Unfortunately, reaction to change is usually negative and typically manifests as resistance, low morale, and low productivity. As a leader, part of your job is to create a motivating atmosphere in support of organizational change.

The first thing you can do is use short-term wins to provide motivation. As short-term wins are achieved, the organization moves closer to realizing the final change objective, which provides evidence that the change effort is worthwhile.

Vision can also help create a supportive atmosphere. One of the best things you can do is seek input from employees when creating vision. This will help build understanding and demonstrate respect, which in turn builds support for the change initiative.

USING SHORT-TERM WINS TO MOTIVATE

Using short-term wins to motivate

As organizational change takes place, employees' feelings are affected. Everyone will react, even you. This is inevitable.

Employees will have different reactions to change – sometimes positive and sometimes negative. You need to manage negative reactions because they can be damaging to the change initiative. The prospect of change can lead employees to experience feelings of anxiety and fear, resulting in low employee morale. When employees feel this way, the impact on the organization is also negative, and usually translates into a loss of productivity.

Sometimes leaders try to avoid dealing with change, thinking employees will adapt regardless of how it's handled. However, this can backfire. Employees are more likely to be resistant when they aren't involved or informed about the change.

On the other hand, when leaders approach change openly and honestly, employees are more likely to be supportive. In addition to being open and honest, you can work to create a motivating atmosphere in support of organizational change. Do this by creating short-term wins and vision.

Short-term wins

Short-term wins, goals that demonstrate progress being made toward achieving the change, focus on the present and help demonstrate that the change is beneficial in the short term too. Alone, the achievement of short-term wins may seem insignificant. Together, each "win" represents achievement of the change. Short-term wins are vital in the change process because they help to motivate individuals toward the final change.

Vision

Creating a vision can provide motivation by helping others understand how the change will impact them and improve the organization. Vision addresses the future and helps people understand where they're going, what's expected of them, and what they're working for.

Short-term wins provide the motivation for the present and near future, while creating a vision provides a clear way forward. Together short-term wins and vision help you build a motivating atmosphere to move the organization closer to achieving the desired change.

Creating vision and short-term wins can also help you gain the political support you need to implement the change. Because short-term wins demonstrate that the initiative is providing benefit and vision is providing guidance, you'll gain and keep the support of leaders within your organization.

Short-term wins can help you avoid a few mistakes commonly made when initiating change. For instance, overlooking short-term realities while pursuing the overall change objective can allow resistance or fear to grow among members of the organization. It may also seem like no progress is being made. Under these circumstances, you run the risk of losing support for the change initiative. To avoid these mistakes, as short term-wins are achieved, use them to celebrate success and build morale and momentum in favor of the change.

Another mistake often made by leaders is not addressing the needs of employees. Employees want to know how the change impacts them in the present, not just when the change is fully implemented. Short-term wins can provide the direction and stability employees need to overcome resistance and support the change.

Question

Benefits of using short-term wins include providing opportunities to celebrate and build morale, motivation, and momentum for change.

Can you think of any others?

Options:

1. Providing evidence that the sacrifices associated with the change are worth it

2. Building your credibility as a leader

3. Undermining cynics

4. Giving resisters a reason to support the change instead

5. Preparing employees for other change initiatives

6. Giving management support for all change initiatives

Answer

Option 1: This option is correct. Sometimes members of the organization question whether the sacrifices that often accompany a change, such as loss of productivity in the short term, will be worth it in the long term.

Option 2: This option is correct. Setting and attaining short-term wins will help build your credibility as a leader capable of leading the organization through change.

Option 3: This option is correct. Achieving short-term wins helps to undermine and win over cynics. As they witness progress toward the final change goal, cynics will likely become supporters.

Option 4: This option is correct. As short-term wins are achieved, resisters will have less reason to resist. Gaining the support of resisters will improve the change's potential for success.

Option 5: This option is incorrect. Short-term wins are directly related to the change initiative at hand. However, achieving them may well have a positive impact throughout the organization.

Option 6: This option is incorrect. It's unrealistic to think that achieving change-specific short-terms wins will help management get support for all other initiatives.

When you create short-term wins, you need them to be effective, if they are to provide any benefit. Short-term wins will be effective if they are realistic, and tangible and indisputable.

Realistic

Realistic short-term wins are achievable in a short period of time and contribute to achieving the ultimate change objective, which builds motivation.

For example, say you have set a short-term win goal to reduce carbon emissions as part of your organization's larger change initiative of reducing its environmental impact. The change initiative is expected to take five years, and the goal of reducing carbon emissions to the specified limit will take at least ten years. This is an inappropriate short-term win because it can't be achieved within a short period of time.

Tangible and indisputable

Tangible and indisputable goals are clearly stated. They describe the desired outcome, according to well-defined criteria, and the time frame or deadline for completion. Vague targets don't make effective short-term wins. And any ambiguity or confusion about what it means to meet a goal can limit its effectiveness, render it useless, or it may even be damaging to the overall change initiative.

For example, "improving cross-sales for game consoles and controllers" is an inappropriate short- term win. This short-term win fails to define what improvement is expected or when it's expected to be achieved.

A company is working on a change initiative to be achieved within the fiscal year and has set some short-term wins. Follow along to find out why these examples are or are not appropriate short-term wins.

Appropriate short-term win: "Reduce costs by 10% this quarter." This is a good short-term win because it can be achieved in the short term, can be measured as a reduction from current costs, and it'll be clear if met, because the target has been defined as a 10% cost reduction.

Inappropriate short-term win: "Increase repair plan sales by 15% by the end of the second quarter." This short-term win is realistic because it can be achieved quickly in relation to the change goal. But, because you don't know what product it applies to, the short-term win is neither tangible nor indisputable.

Managing Organizational Change

Question
Which are good examples of short-term wins?
Options:
1. Achieve a reduction in the number of abandoned calls this month compared to last month
2. Implement a peer-nomination system by the end of this quarter
3. Establish an employee recognition committee within two months
4. Introduce a newly designed version of the crossover SUV to target a younger customer base
5. Develop best-practice guidelines for all service call booking procedures within one month, and use experienced customer service representatives to provide input

Answer
Option 1: This option is correct. A reduction in abandoned calls is achievable in the short term, and everyone knows that achieving the goal requires the number of abandoned calls to be lowered.

Option 2: This option is correct. This short-term win is achievable in a short time period, which makes it realistic. It's also tangible and indisputable – you know what needs to be done and by when.

Option 3: This option is correct. This short-term win will be achieved in a short time period and defines what it means for the goal to be achieved.

Option 4: This option is incorrect. Introducing a new crossover SUV does not meet any of the criteria for being a short-term win. You have no idea if this can be achieved quickly to act as a motivator, and you have no way of measuring progress or knowing when the goal is achieved.

Option 5: This option is incorrect. There's no way of knowing if developing best-practice guidelines for service calls is a realistic short-term win. The short-term win also fails to provide a way to measure results or tell objectively when the goal has been achieved.

USING VISION TO BUILD SUPPORT FOR CHANGE

Using vision to build support for change
Great leaders have great vision. You'll need to be able to create vision too, if you want to successfully lead your organization, unit, or team through change.

Just as short-term wins help provide motivation and build support for a change, so too can creating and sharing a vision of the future. Involving employees in the process of creating vision will also help them embrace the change by helping them understand how it will impact them and the organization.

Educating employees about the change will help alleviate the uncertainty often brought on by change, helping to gain their support.

Involving employees
Perhaps above all else, employees want to feel respected. Involving them in creating a vision demonstrates that, as a leader, you value their contribution and recognize their input will improve the effectiveness and success of the change effort.

Use three simple guidelines when creating vision. An effective vision will create support for change by clearly depicting what the organization is trying to accomplish, being realistic, and including input from employees.

Clearly depict what the organization is trying to accomplish

Your vision must depict clearly what the organization is trying to accomplish through the change initiative. Create a vision that explains how the change will reshape the organization. What problem will it solve, or what aspect of work quality of life will it address? Be sure to tell what direction the organization is heading in and how the change affects employees, both now and when the change objective is achieved. A clear description will help ensure all members of the organization are working toward the same goal.

Be realistic

Make sure your vision is realistic. If employees can't support your vision because they don't believe it's realistic, you'll never gain their support. Cynicism and resistance can grow if your vision for the change effort is not realistic.

Include input from employees

Including input from employees will help gain their support for the change. Employees possess a wealth of knowledge and information, and if you get them involved with creating the vision, the change effort will benefit from their expertise. It also helps to show respect and value for employees, which is a vital part of gaining support. Involving them will help them feel more confident about the change.

Question

Managing Organizational Change

Which are guidelines for creating a vision to support organizational change?
Options:
1. Depict clearly what the organization is trying to accomplish
2. Be realistic
3. Include input from employees
4. Prove that the change initiative will work
5. Use industry standards to guide your vision

Answer

Option 1: This option is correct. Your vision should define what it is the organization is trying to accomplish with the change initiative. This provides direction for all members of the organization, helping to make sure everyone understands what they're working for.

Option 2: This option is correct. Your vision must be realistic if it's going to help build support for the change initiative.

Option 3: This option is correct. When creating your vision, you'd be wise to include input from people throughout the organization. Showing respect for the employees by asking for their input will win support for the change.

Option 4: This option is incorrect. Your vision needs to be realistic and depict what it is the organization is trying to accomplish. Expecting the vision to prove that the change will work as intended is overzealous.

Option 5: This option is incorrect. Unless the change is intended to bring your organization in line with industry standards, this won't help create an effective vision.

SECTION 2 - LISTENING TO EMPLOYEES DURING CHANGE

SECTION 2 - Listening to Employees during Change

As a leader, you need to support your employees during change. To do this, while also building support for the change initiative, you need to understand what employees are feeling and thinking.

Use a four-step listening technique to help you accomplish this: encourage open communication, "listen" to your employees' feelings, check for understanding, and take their input on board.

EFFECTIVE LISTENING

Effective listening

During the change process, everyone reacts to change and everyone has an opinion – that's just human nature. However, it's how you handle reactions to, and opinions about change that will impact the success of the change initiative.

People often find change exciting – new challenges and new ways to do things – but sometimes they react negatively. When reactions to change are negative, opinions may come off as complaints or criticism. Successfully leading your employees through change involves managing their reactions and accepting their input in a way that builds support for the initiative.

Build mutual understanding and support for change using open communication and active listening. As employees share their feelings and opinions, you can help them view the change in a positive way. Active listening will help you convey concern, interest, and respect, which in turn enhances open communication.

However, listening to your employees isn't enough. You must be prepared to act on their input, if appropriate. You need to demonstrate that you respect and value their suggestions and determine whether they should be implemented.

A four-step listening technique can help you build support for change initiatives with your employees. You should encourage open communication, "listen" to your employees' feelings, check for understanding, and take their input on board.

In step one, you encourage open communication to learn how your employees feel about the change initiative. Once you know how they feel, you can help them view the change more positively, which will help build support. Begin with a question inviting employees to share their feelings.

Guidelines to help you encourage open communication include asking questions, and being open, honest, positive, and sensitive.

A few things to avoid when encouraging open communication include being judgmental, dismissive, or assuming to know how someone is feeling.

Question

Kareem's organization just embarked on a change initiative and he's talking with one of his employees, Natalie, about how it's affecting her.

What might Kareem say to Natalie to encourage open communication?

Options:
1. "How are you feeling about the change?"
2. "Are you overreacting like everyone else?"
3. "I suppose you're feeling incompetent."

Answer

Option 1: This is the correct option. By asking Natalie how she feels, Kareem is showing he cares and is encouraging her to speak openly.

Option 2: This option is incorrect. This response is dismissive. Natalie is not likely to share openly now.

Option 3: This option is incorrect. Kareem shouldn't assume to know how Natalie feels. After an opening like this, she's probably offended and disinterested in communicating.

In step two of the listening technique, you "listen" to your employees' feelings by restating in your own words the feelings they've expressed. This helps establish empathy.

When restating your employee's feelings, follow these simple, yet effective guidelines:

- do continue to encourage open communication, and
- don't judge, make assumptions, or be dismissive.

Recall that Kareem asked Natalie how she's feeling about a change initiative. Follow along as Kareem "listens" to her feelings.

Natalie: Well, I'm optimistic but worried. I'm afraid we won't be able to learn to use all the features of the new machinery fast enough.

Kareem: So, if I understand correctly, you're afraid the team won't be able to learn to use the new machinery in the time available.

Natalie: Exactly.

Kareem: Well, there's nothing that can be done about that. The team will just have to learn fast.

Natalie: Oh alright, I guess.

Kareem restated Natalie's feelings without adding any of his own feelings, which is great. But then Kareem dropped the ball when he dismissed Natalie's concern by stating that nothing could be done.

After telling you their feelings, employees may have an opinion to express. When input is offered, you need to check for understanding, which is step three in effective listening. Summarizing and restating input is an effective way to do this.

Do

As you check for understanding, ask questions, demonstrate you're listening by restating – in your own words – the concern expressed, invite input on how to resolve problems or address concerns, and take employees seriously.

Don't

When checking for understanding, don't judge or make assumptions, prejudge how a situation can be resolved, become defensive, interrupt with a rebuttal, ignore criticism, be dismissive, or impose your own views.

Question

Now that Natalie has shared her feelings, she has a concern she'd like to express. She thinks the new equipment is calibrated improperly and needs to be checked by the manufacturer.

Which statements are examples of things Kareem could say to check his understanding of Natalie's input?

Options:

1. "Oh really, can you tell me what makes you think that?"

2. "You believe the equipment needs to be recalibrated, right?"

3. "It can't be that bad; the equipment is brand new."
4. "Thanks Natalie, but I don't think you're qualified to make such an assertion."

Answer

Option 1: This option is correct. Asking leading questions will help Kareem gain more insight. It also demonstrates interest and lets Natalie know he's taking her input seriously.

Option 2: This option is correct. Restating what Natalie said in his own words is a great way for Kareem to establish understanding, and demonstrate he's been listening. It also offers a chance for correction.

Option 3: This option is incorrect. Kareem's dismissiveness makes it seem as though he doesn't trust Natalie's input or take it seriously.

Option 4: This option is incorrect. Kareem's dismissiveness and lack of respect will likely stop Natalie from sharing any more input.

In step four of the listening technique, you take employees' input on board. You need to act on input by determining if it should be implemented. Some input will be relevant and some won't. Either way, you need to follow up with the individual and explain why the input is or isn't being implemented. This demonstrates respect and confirms for the employee that their input was taken seriously and is valued.

You'll want to make sure you do certain things when taking input on board: be willing to act
- investigate the input,
- wrap things up on a positive note, and
- thank the employee for the input.

And when taking your employees' input on board, it's unacceptable to do nothing or to ignore it. Always acting on input will encourage your employees to continue to share valuable insight with you.

Remember that Natalie spoke to Kareem regarding a concern about using new machinery, but she hasn't heard anything further. Follow along to find out what happens when they run into each other at work.

Natalie: Hey Kareem, so what did you find out?

Kareem: About?

Natalie: My concern with the new machinery.

Kareem: Oh right. I actually didn't follow up on it. I don't think anyone is open to making more changes right now. So instead of rocking the boat, I just dropped it.

Natalie: Ah, OK then.

Kareem handled this all wrong. He should have investigated Natalie's input. And whatever the outcome, he should have provided feedback. A "thank-you" would have been a nice way to wrap things up.

Question

Mario is speaking with one of his employees, Thomas, about a change initiative. Thomas starts by expressing his feelings, "I'm anxious about the new procedure. There just hasn't been enough communication about it for me to be comfortable." Then he says, "Based on my experience, I think this new procedure includes some redundant steps that will actually take more time than the old procedure."

Match each step of the listening technique to the example that demonstrates Mario using it appropriately.

Options:

A. Encourage open communication

B. "Listen" to your employees' feelings

C. Check for understanding
D. Take their input on board

Targets:

1. "How do you feel about the way the change is progressing?"

2. "I can understand you're anxious because communication hasn't been adequate."

3. "So, you're concerned the new procedure will actually take more time?"

4. "I've looked into it, and you're absolutely right. We've identified adjustments we can make to recapture that lost time."

Answer

Asking employees to share their feelings encourages open communication and will give you the insight you need to help them deal with their feelings.

Restating an employee's feelings in your own words demonstrates you've been listening.

When an employee offers input about a change, you need to check that you understand correctly. Part of taking action on input is closing the feedback loop with the employee involved.

SECTION 3 - SUPPORTING INDIVIDUALS THROUGH CHANGE

SECTION 3 - Supporting Individuals through Change

Supporting individuals through change is an essential part of leading during a change initiative. By supporting your employees, you'll in turn be creating support for the organizational change.

Support individuals through change initiatives by coaching and empowering them. Coaching involves encouraging autonomy, continual development, and ownership and responsibility. Empowering employees involves preparing employees for success, factoring in each employee's qualities and attitudes when redesigning roles and assigning responsibilities, and being flexible.

COACHING FOR CHANGE

Coaching for change

When organizational change happens, shifts in power, responsibilities, and functions are likely. The success of the change initiative will depend partly on the ability of individuals to adapt. This is especially true if the change substantially alters or redefines jobs, roles, functions, daily activities, or responsibilities.

As a leader, you need to continue to build support for the change, and part of this is supporting individuals as they adapt to the change. Coaching and empowering employees are great ways to support individuals through change.

Effective coaching is based on partnership, not instruction or orders. This means you need to treat employees as partners, not subordinates. Coaching is about being committed to your employees' growth, and is a way to demonstrate that they are valued.

To develop good coaching relationships with your employees, open communication and trust are imperative. The three elements of a good coaching partnership are autonomy, continual development, and ownership and responsibility.

Autonomy

Encourage autonomy by allowing your employees to make decisions. Your job as a coach is to listen as employees discuss their ideas. You can even brainstorm with them, but don't give orders or instructions. If mistakes are made, you can discuss what went wrong and support employees as they resolve the issue.

Continual development

Learning is integral to successful change. And you can promote continual development as a way for employees to adapt to the changed demands of their jobs. Examples of ways you can encourage continual development are establishing new standards or guidelines, reviewing accomplishments, and looking for ways to improve how things are done.

Ownership and responsibility

During change, it's crucial that you don't take responsibility away from employees. Instead, encourage employees to take ownership of all aspects of their work. Let them do the work and trust in their ability to achieve. Of course, if they turn to you for guidance, you can support them through coaching.

Eleanor is leading her team of insurance consultants through a change initiative designed to bring the company in line with strict government regulation. Follow along as Eleanor relies on coaching to support some of her employees.

Autonomy: Jeff and Eleanor are meeting in her office. He's working with a large company to close an insurance deal and he wants Eleanor to choose a course of action.

Managing Organizational Change

Instead, Eleanor encourages Jeff to share his thoughts with her. She helps him work through his ideas. By the time Jeff leaves her office, he has made up his own mind about how to proceed.

Continual development: Ling approaches Eleanor, expressing her concern that she won't be able to learn the new procedures that support the government guidelines. Eleanor provides Ling with information about the guidelines. She encourages Ling to study the guidelines and to come back if she needs help understanding them.

Ownership and responsibility: As part of the change initiative, Eleanor has assigned Redmond the task of determining how to ensure compliance. Redmond is considering several approaches to a compliance issue and expects Eleanor to tell him what to do. But instead of telling him what to do, she suggests he do it his way. She tells him "I'm sure you're in the best position to know what's right. I trust your ability."

Eleanor understands the importance of coaching her employees. She was careful to encourage autonomy when Jeff asked her to make a decision about his work. She provided resources and offered to help Ling learn the new guidelines, which will help Ling do her job. And she encouraged ownership and responsibility when she suggested Redmond do things his own way.

Through coaching, Eleanor was able to help her employees adapt to the change, and strengthen her relationships with them.

Question

Coaching for change is part of supporting employees during change.

What elements should be encouraged as part of a successful coaching relationship?

Options:

1. Allow employees to make decisions
2. Provide opportunity for growth in support of the change
3. Hold employees accountable for their work
4. Identify potential problems and dictate their resolution
5. Tell employees how to proceed with their work

Answer

Option 1: This option is correct. Encouraging autonomy helps support employees through change by helping them learn while still moving toward achieving the change.

Option 2: This option is correct. Encouraging continual development is a great way to support employees. Help them learn what they need to know to continue to perform their job.

Option 3: This option is correct. Encouraging ownership and responsibility supports employees through change by telling them you trust them and have faith in their ability to handle the changes.

Option 4: This option is not correct. Coaching is not about telling your employees what to do. You need to support them, not do their job for them.

Option 5: This option is not correct. Good coaching relationships are based on partnership, not dictatorship. Promote autonomy by allowing employees to make their own decisions.

SUPPORTING FOR CHANGE

Supporting for change

In addition to coaching, you can support your employees through change by helping them successfully adapt to the change. You can do this by preparing employees for success, factoring in each employee's qualities and attitudes when redesigning roles and assigning responsibilities, and being flexible.

Preparing employees for success means that you ensure your employees can do their jobs in the changed organization.

It's your job make sure your employees have the knowledge and skills necessary to successfully implement and perform what's expected of them.

If your employees are unprepared to fulfill their roles, they can feel helpless and confused, which can leave them demotivated and resistant to change. And of course, you want to avoid anything that might negatively impact the success of the organizational change.

Frank is involved in a change initiative. His organization is doing some restructuring in an attempt to improve productivity. Frank decides to first identify the critical knowledge and skills his employees will need to implement the change.

Once he's done, he reviews his employees' files to determine what experience and skills each person has. Based on this, he can follow up with each of them and design a plan to get them ready to fulfill their new job requirements.

Another thing you can do to support employees through the change initiative is factor in each employee's qualities and attitudes when redesigning roles and assigning responsibilities. This just makes good sense.

If part of the change initiative requires you to redefine job descriptions or assign new responsibilities, employees will adapt quicker and be more supportive if you align roles and responsibilities with individual preferences, qualities, and attitudes.

Even better, if you can, assign roles and responsibilities to appeal to a person's interests or preferred career advancement. These interests may include a new position or new responsibilities in the future.

Frank has just reviewed personnel files and has spoken to his employees. The change initiative will require some juggling of roles and responsibilities. Follow along as Frank discusses who he will assign to what roles and why.

Frank: Who can I assign to the task of redesigning the workflow to achieve the desired efficiencies? Lita is very knowledgeable about the existing process and has Kaizen experience. Also, she's very dedicated, which will help when times get tough, as I expect they will.

Frank: I also need someone to write up new procedures. Perhaps Edward – he has mentioned wanting to move into a technical support role. I know he has experience with technical writing and won't use highly technical language so the resulting procedures will be accessible.

Frank: And who would be right for the training role? I know, I'll approach Gerald. He's always helping his teammates solve problems. And he does have a teaching degree and a positive attitude.

Finally, being flexible about how the employees adapt to the change will help them be more positive and accepting of it. One of the reasons that employees react negatively to change is that they feel pressured into working in new ways. Flexibility can help you avoid this.

Be flexible when you redefine job roles and, if possible, give employees some control. For instance, allow employees to alter their working hours, practices, or conditions. How you use these methods to empower employees will depend on the actual situation and the individuals concerned.

Frank knows his employees will be more accepting of the change if they have some control over it. He calls a team meeting to discuss the possibilities. His employees are relieved to know there's some flexibility in transitioning and adapting to the organizational change.

Question

In addition to coaching, what else can you do to support individuals through change?

Options:

1. Make sure employees have requisite knowledge to perform in new roles

2. Assign roles based on individual preferences

3. Give employees freedom to accommodate the change as it suits them

4. Let employees abstain from participating in the change

5. Provide detailed guidelines for successfully adapting to the change

Answer

Option 1: This option is correct. You need to make sure your employees are able to do their jobs. This helps alleviate anxiety and promotes successful organizational change.

Option 2: This option is correct. The more you can do to accommodate the individual, the better. This will provide incentive for the individual to support the change.

Option 3: This option is correct. Having some control over the change and how they choose to adapt to it can reduce employees' resistance to change.

Option 4: This option is incorrect. All employees need to be involved, otherwise they won't embrace or support the change.

Option 5: This option is incorrect. Employees should be encouraged, when possible, to choose how they adapt to the demands of the change.

CHAPTER 3 - DEALING WITH RESISTANCE TO CHANGE

CHAPTER 3 - Dealing with Resistance to Change
   SECTION 1 - Symptoms of Resistance to Change
   SECTION 2 - Roots of Resistance to Change
   SECTION 3 - Handling Resistance to Change

SECTION 1 - SYMPTOMS OF RESISTANCE TO CHANGE

SECTION 1 - Symptoms of Resistance to Change

Resistance to change has sources and symptoms. The sources are the thinking and feeling elements of resistance. The symptoms are the behaviors that result from a person's thoughts and feelings about the change.

Negative sources such as fear or anxiety can lead to active or passive dysfunctional behaviors. Constructive resistance stems from an employee's concern for the organization and can be used as a positive force.

RESISTANCE TO CHANGE

Resistance to change

Change dominates the modern business landscape. All organizations – large or small – deal with change brought about by innovation, reorganization, advanced technologies, market shifts, new product lines, and other influences. Ultimately, an organization's success depends on how well managers handle the most important element of change – people.

Change can fail – not because of its worth, but because of how well that change is accepted by those who are affected by it. In its simplest interpretation, resistance is anything that slows or stops movement, or that keeps movement from happening.

In business, resistance is dysfunctional behavior triggered by an emotional or belief-based reaction to change.

Where managing change begins

Overcoming resistance to change begins with your management skills. It's virtually impossible to lead your employees if you don't have the ability to embrace change yourself. Demonstrating your commitment to the change process will provide the positive energy needed to counteract resistance.

Managing change means managing resistance as well. If you anticipate and recognize resistance, you can learn to use it to create support.

Businesses are constantly changing, and employees are frequently required to adapt to changes and learn new ways to do things. New staff members, updated equipment, training programs, and promotions are usually greeted with interest and acceptance.

However, this is not always the case. There are times when employees begin to display dysfunctional behavior in reaction to change. This is the point where resistance begins. People resist change for many reasons, including fear, misunderstanding, anxiety, resentment, hostility, subversion, or lack of trust.

The cost to businesses is high. Initiatives crash or have costly overruns. Projects fail to meet requirements. Customers are lost to competitors.

But If the cost of mishandling resistance is high for organizations, it's equally as high for employees. Even if a previous change was ultimately successful, employees may be left with a bitter taste. They may become resentful, apathetic, or fearful of trying new things. At worst, they may abandon the organization for somewhere they feel more accepted and valued.

Resistance is simply reactive behavior. Managing your employees' resistance to change involves determining both its sources and its symptoms. Select each element of resistance for more information.

Sources

The sources of resistance are your employees' perceptions of change – the beliefs and emotions that color their judgment. Sources are the roots from which the symptoms of resistance grow.

Symptoms

The symptoms of resistance are your employees' reactions to the change. Symptoms involve dysfunctional behaviors that result when employees react to the sources of resistance.

SYMPTOMS OF RESISTANCE

Symptoms of resistance

Reaction to change in an organization is directly linked to a person's perception of its personal impact. This means symptoms of resistance can be found at every level of an organization.

But despite their far-reaching impact, dysfunctional behaviors generally fall into two categories of resistance to change: passive resistance and active resistance.

ACTIVE AND PASSIVE RESISTANCE

Active and passive resistance
Active resistance involves overtly challenging change. Active resisters push back against change efforts by openly disagreeing and actively lobbying against the change effort. A number of dysfunctional behaviors are associated with active resistance to change.
Finding fault
Resisters may find fault with change by complaining about or ridiculing the change. This can be done directly by speaking up at meetings, or covertly through gossiping and spreading rumors.
Manipulation
Manipulators control situations through influence. They may resist change through the selective use of facts to back their cause, or by consciously structuring events to fail.
Rallying
Rallying involves garnering support from others for resistance to change. Ralliers may create an "us against them" situation, polarizing workers against management.

Or they may indulge in fearmongering – inducing apprehension in coworkers by stressing or exaggerating negative effects of the change.

Malicious compliance

Malicious, or letter-of-the-law, compliance involves meeting the minimum requirements of change implementation, while purposely ignoring the spirit and intent of what that change is supposed to achieve.

Passive resistance is silent opposition to change. Unlike active resistance, which involves action, passive resistance involves inaction. Rather than challenging or actively blocking change, employees involved in passive resistance simply ignore or don't participate in the change effort.

Because passive resistance is intangible, dysfunctional behaviors are more difficult to detect.

Avoiding commitment

Employees may resist change by avoiding any genuine commitment. If confronted, they respond with statements like "No one told me" or "I never said I'd do that."

Benign neglect

Benign neglect involves appearing to agree with the change, but not following through with any support. When questioned, employees may feign ignorance, or find reasons to procrastinate taking action.

Imposing sanctions

Imposing sanctions involves controlling or withholding effort, information, or resources that are needed for the change. Employees may restrict access to office equipment, or may hoard budget resources needed for the change effort. Or they may slow down work output to minimal levels as a silent protest.

Pursuing business as usual

Some employees resist moving out of their comfort zones and trying new things. They continue to pursue business as usual, doing things "the way we always have."

A large urban hospital has instituted a new system for handling paperwork and files. Geoffrey and Danielle are clerks in the records office. Follow along for an example of each type of resistance.

Passive: Geoffrey exhibits passive resistance. When the new system is implemented, Geoffrey says nothing, but slows down his pace of work and gets fewer and fewer reports filed.

Active: Danielle exhibits active resistance. She sends a pile of files back to her supervisor with a note saying that she's too busy with the difficult new system and that someone else will have to deal with the files in order to meet the deadline.

CONSTRUCTIVE RESISTANCE

Constructive resistance
So, change is coming and it's up to you to make it happen. After all, your way is the right way, and employees will need to be persuaded or made to go along with it. Right?

Before you decide that any type of resistance is a negative force, you should step back and consider the nature of that resistance. Perhaps it's something to be to be utilized, not overcome. Sometimes you have to bring resistant people along by addressing their needs. In this way, resistance can play a useful role in change management.

Remember, your employees have valuable experience. When they question or critique change, they may be exhibiting constructive resistance – resistance motivated by their desire to collaborate on a change solution. This can be valuable to the change effort. Your employees may know things about costs involved, issues that lie ahead, and creative possibilities that you haven't thought of.

Managing Organizational Change

Constructive resistance is motivated by an individual's desire to protect the best interests of the organization. Employees that express constructive resistance bring with them the energy and motivation needed to implement change.

These employees want a "win-win" situation – to trade their commitment for your answers to their questions, concerns, and desires. Examples of constructive resistance include constructive critique, asking procedural questions, offering assistance, conditional agreement, and bargaining.

You're the general manager of a large financial services firm. The organization has recently hired an IT firm to implement an extensive new information management system. Follow along as three department managers demonstrate constructive resistance to the change.

Vijay: This new system is complicated, but I can handle it with some additional training. I've got some ideas for changes to the existing budget that would benefit us both.

Renée: My staff members are unhappy about being told how to do their jobs by an outside company. I know they'll accept the technology, but you'll need to let me handle the communication during the implementation phase of the project.

Aaron: I've gone over the new system, but I'm not sure that it's going to adequately protect our customers' privacy. I'd like to arrange a meeting so we can go over the questions and concerns I have.

The three employees at the financial services firm were each motivated by the desire to make things better. Vijay offered a bargain that would be mutually beneficial.

Involving him in a win-win situation will solidify his commitment and make him feel positive about the change.

Renée was experienced enough to realize her staff could be a problem if not handled correctly. By relying on her experience and actively involving her in the change, you'll gain her support. Aaron needed more information before he could commit to the change. Responding to his concerns will help build a constructive relationship and secure his commitment to the change.

Question

A large urban community college is initiating an innovative e-learning program that would allow students to take courses online. Some of the teaching staff are resistant to the new program.

Match the type of resistance to a behavioral example.

Options:

A. Active resistance
B. Passive resistance
C. Constructive resistance

Targets:

1. Hope sends an e-mail to her fellow teachers claiming that the change could lead to staff layoffs

2. Diego continually arranges his teaching schedule to conflict with the e-learning training sessions he's been asked to attend

3. Trish suggests that the college communicate the details of how teachers will be compensated for their intellectual contributions to the courseware

Answer

Hope is demonstrating active resistance because she's openly disagreeing and actively lobbying against the change effort.

Diego's avoidance of the change effort is an example of passive resistance.

Trish's constructive resistance is motivated by the desire to collaborate on a change solution.

SOURCES OF RESISTANCE

Sources of resistance

The symptoms of resistance are your employees' reactive behaviors to change. But what causes those behaviors? Why are people so resistant to change? To deal with resistance to change, you have to determine its sources - the roots of where the resistance is coming from – and why this can cause negative behavior.

The sources of resistance are people's emotional and intellectual responses – how they think and feel about change. This is what ultimately determines how they will behave.

One of the main sources of resistance is the underlying fear and anxiety caused by uncertainty about the change. For example, employees may fear the change is going to negatively affect their status, position, or authority.

Sometimes employees believe the change is inequitable and benefits others more than themselves. They rationalize the change isn't worthy of acceptance.

Another reason may be an emotional reaction to the method by which the change is introduced. For example, if you use an authoritarian approach, it may be perceived as bullying and result in a push- back reaction from employees.

The large urban community college is proceeding with the implementation of its new e-learning program. The project must be completed before the start of the new school year to allow students to register.

The project manager is determined to meet the deadline and avoid delaying the project for another year. He sends out detailed information to his teachers delegating responsibilities and timelines for submitting content for the courses.

Although the project seems to start well, it soon begins to fall behind schedule. The teachers are slow to provide requested material for the courses, and the content they do provide doesn't match what was requested. The problems soon add up, and the project is delayed for another year. So what went wrong?

The problem at the community college was that the project manager concentrated his efforts on the operational integrity of the project and didn't pay attention to the roots of resistance to change. Follow along as two of the college teachers express the fears that are causing them to resist change.

Hope: This new project is a deliberate attempt to get rid of classrooms. I've talked to the rest of the staff and they agree with me.

Diego: The way I teach has always been good enough. Why should I help make myself obsolete?

Question

What do you think are the benefits of going to the source of a problem to deal with resistance to change?

Options:
1. You'll reduce or eliminate the symptoms of resistance
2. You'll help employees feel positive about the change
3. You'll promote positive and accurate beliefs about the change
4. You'll have an easier time getting employees to accept and adapt to the change
5. You'll be able to make sure staff members go along with the way you want to do things
6. You'll be able to eliminate dissent among your employees

Answer

Option 1: This option is correct. The symptoms of resistance – dysfunctional behaviors – spring from the sources of resistance – emotional and intellectual responses to change.

Option 2: This option is correct. By addressing the emotional component of resistance at the source, you'll help secure commitment to the change before problems escalate into negative behavior.

Option 3: This option is correct. Resistant behavior often stems from negative beliefs about the effects of the change.

Option 4: This option is correct. When employees understand and feel good about the change from the beginning, they'll be more likely to accept and adapt to new ways of doing things.

Option 5: This option is incorrect. Sometimes employees have legitimate reasons for concern. You should consider why they think and feel the way they do.

Option 6: This option is incorrect. The purpose is to eliminate dysfunction, not dissent. When dissent stems from a constructive concern for the organization, it can be a valuable resource.

SECTION 2 - ROOTS OF RESISTANCE TO CHANGE

SECTION 2 - Roots of Resistance to Change

Resistance is rooted in your employees' emotional and intellectual reactions to change. This resistance can manifest in feelings or beliefs such as fear, close-mindedness, skepticism, or powerlessness.

A number of existing conditions or circumstances within organizations can also exacerbate resistance in employees. Timing your change efforts with these conditions in mind can temper their influence on employees' resistance to change.

WHY PEOPLE RESIST CHANGE

Why people resist change

You've met them – employees whose resistance to change is impeding progress. They may object loudly to anyone that will listen or simply sit in at meetings without offering any input. Perhaps they withhold resources, are slow to alter their work routines, or use subversion to sabotage your initiatives. But despite their approach, these employees have one thing in common – they're rejecting the opportunity to learn, grow, help, participate, or make a difference.

The nature of change

So why do people resist change? Well, much of the time they don't. New experiences, adventure, education, responsibility, love, reward, and friendship all involve change. These aren't only accepted by people, they're pursued. People only resist change when it's perceived as a threat rather than an opportunity.

To discover what causes your employees to resist change, you'll need to understand their emotional and intellectual reactions to change – why they think and feel the way they do. Resistance to change is often rooted in four main reactions: fear, close-mindedness, skepticism, and powerlessness.

The four main roots of resistance to change evoke both emotional and intellectual reactions in employees.

Fear

Resistance to change is often rooted in fear. Fearful employees feel it's safer to stay where they are than to move forward, especially if what they are doing is working well for them, and the road ahead is unknown.

Close-mindedness

Close-minded employees cling to the comfort of routine. Asking them to change the way they do things pulls them out of their comfort zone. They firmly believe change is disruptive and unnecessary.

Skepticism

Some employees are skeptical that change will have any positive effect. They may have been through unsuccessful initiatives, or feel they've been "burned" by change in the past. Skepticism may also arise from lack of knowledge or misguided assumptions about the change.

Powerlessness

People resent being asked to change without any understanding of why. Employees may feel powerless because their accepted realities have suddenly shifted.

Question

The first main root of resistance to change is fear. Think of a time when fear of a change at work made you feel resistant. What were you most afraid of?

Options:
1. Failure
2. Uncertainty

3. Loss
Answer

Option 1: It's natural to fear failure. You may have felt your work skills were not up to the change, or that your self-worth was being threatened.

Option 2: Your fear of uncertainty was probably produced because the change threatened your expectations about the future.

Option 3: Fear of loss is a common reaction. Perhaps you felt the change threatened to take away or destroy something of value to you.

Embracing change means adapting to a new way of doing things. Fear of failure can intensify the anxieties people have about their work capabilities.

No one is completely immune to fear of failure. It can affect any employee in your organization who is faced with changing work duties.

Successful employees fear they won't be as effective if they have to change the way they do things. Unconfident or timid employees may become paralyzed by self-doubt.

Have you ever been lost? If so, do you remember how unsettling it was to be neither here nor there, but at some uncertain place in between? Some employees feel the same way about change. They have a sense of control when they're familiar with their work environment, and they may resist trading what they know for an uncertain future. Fear of uncertainty is particularly acute when there's insufficient communication about change – what's happening and what the impact will be.

Fear of loss is one of the most personal emotions people experience in reaction to change. Many employees fear losing their status in the work hierarchy. Employees whose self-worth rests with specialized knowledge may fear change will make them obsolete.

Employees operating within predictable routines also value their support systems. When the change brings a shift in organizational structure, they may fear that new colleagues won't understand them or that new supervisors are predisposed to let them fail.

The second main root of resistance to change is close-mindedness. The predisposition to embrace change varies from person to person. Some people enjoy new opportunities, but others take more persuading. And some people resist change because they're close-minded.

What close-mindedness means

People are described as being close-minded when their minds are closed to new things. Some are just unwilling to bend or are intolerant of the beliefs of others. Some may be suffering from burnout or fatigue, particularly if the road to change has been a long one. Close-minded employees are unwilling to learn or accept the benefits that change could bring. Examples of close-minded employees are those who are unwilling to change work routines or those who cling to old habits.

The third main root of resistance to change is skepticism. Employees are valuable to an organization because of what they know, and how they use their experience to do their job. So it doesn't make sense to shut them out of the change process.

Skeptical employees have sincerely held concerns about the change process. They may react by doubting, questioning, and disagreeing with you about the goals of the change or how it's being implemented.

It's important to communicate openly and honestly with skeptical employees. Skeptics often exert influence over their coworkers because they're perceived as having the courage of their convictions.

Skepticism can be rooted in false assumptions about what the effects of the change will be. For example, a financial services company is implementing metrics to go along with a new information management system.

Aaron

"As far as I can tell, these new customer service metrics are just like the old ones. Why should I put time and effort into something that didn't work the last time we tried it?"

Renée

"I haven't heard anything about retraining to go along with these new metrics. It seems like this change is just an excuse to weed out the long-term members on staff. I can't be a part of that."

The fourth main root of resistance to change is powerlessness. Would you step onto a busy street without looking where you were going? Of course not. That would be dangerous. Just as with that busy street, the first reaction to workplace change is usually caution. This can be positive – caution allows people to think about and assess change before they react. But when employees feel powerless to control their own path, they can become emotionally paralyzed and unable to move beyond caution to understanding and acceptance.

This feeling of powerlessness can be particularly acute when there has been a lack of communication about the effects that change will bring. Employees may dig in their heels when they are caught off guard by change. They may feel that their power in the workplace is being stripped away, or that their skills and knowledge will not be up to the challenge.

Question

You're a manager at a graphic design company that is transitioning to a digital format for layout work. Arman is a senior designer who is resisting the change. He's upset that he wasn't consulted about the change and is refusing to use the new design software. He's openly voicing his opinion that the old way of creating designs strictly on paper is better. Which roots of resistance are evident in Arman's impressions of the change?

Options:

1. Fear
2. Close-mindedness
3. Skepticism
4. Powerlessness

Answer

Option 1: This option is incorrect. Arman is openly resistant and doesn't show fear of the change. His resistance is rooted in an unwillingness to accept what he can't control.

Option 2: This option is correct. Arman shows an unwillingness to change his work routines. This indicates his resistance is rooted in close-mindedness.

Option 3: This option is incorrect. Skepticism is rooted in disbelief that the change will work, or have any positive effects. Arman's resistance is rooted in his unwillingness to accept the change, not in any belief it wouldn't work.

Option 4: This option is correct. Arman expresses that the change was a management decision beyond his control. This indicates his resistance is rooted in a feeling of powerlessness.

CONDITIONS THAT BREED RESISTANCE

Conditions that breed resistance

When you're dealing with resistance to change, keep in mind that it's not a personal attack. Resistance is rooted in the circumstances of the change. Your employees are demonstrating a rejection of the change process, not of you. When you deal with your employees' emotions, it's important to keep your own in check.

It's also important not to jump right in to action when you're dealing with change. You'll need to consider that other forces can hamper your change initiatives. You may have to deal with existing conditions or circumstances within the organization that can exacerbate resistance in your employees.

Although sometimes difficult to control, it's important to be aware of these conditions, and their potential to sabotage your change efforts.

The timing of change efforts in relation to other conditions may also increase your employees' resistance to change. Poor timing can mean the difference between success and failure. Sometimes a change that would normally have no ill effect can stir up an emotional reaction when timed badly.

For example, consider a retail store that is setting up a new department to deal with online shopping. The company hires several new employees to set up and maintain the new computer systems.

Unfortunately, the hiring coincides with a number of layoffs in the Marketing and Sales Departments. Even though the changes are not connected, many staff members perceive that long-term employees are being terminated to make way for the new workers.

Cooperation with the staff of the new department is minimal at best. The project fails to meet its implementation deadline, resulting in severe budget overruns.

Question

A fast food restaurant is initiating a new program to decrease wait times and increase customer service. A number of employees are resisting the change.

Match each root of resistance to the employee statement that best exemplifies it. Each root matches to one statement. There will be two statements that will not have a match.

Options:

A. Skepticism
B. Fear

Targets:

1. "This new program is just a fad. They do something like this every year and it never lasts."

2. "I'll never be able to learn this new system. I just know they're going to fire me."

Managing Organizational Change

3. "I'm not reading that new training manual. I already know all I need to about serving customers."

4. "Nobody asked me what I think. So I really don't care one way or another if this succeeds."

Answer

You should review the roots of resistance.

Skeptical employees are resistant to change because they just don't believe it's going to have any lasting or beneficial effect.

Fearful employees may worry that the change threatens something of value to them or that they won't have the skills to cope.

This statement is evidence of close-mindedness, not fear or skepticism. The employee is refusing to consider other options.

This statement is evidence of powerlessness, not fear or skepticism. The employee is demonstrating a lack of control over the change.

SECTION 3 - HANDLING RESISTANCE TO CHANGE

SECTION 3 - Handling Resistance to Change

Handling resistance to change involves understanding the beliefs and emotions that influence how your employees approach change. You can use several techniques for dealing with resistance, including using open communication, employee involvement, and change agents.

DEALING WITH RESISTANCE

Dealing with resistance

To handle resistance, you'll have to understand the factors that influence how your employees approach change – the beliefs they hold, their emotional frames of reference, their relationships with you and their coworkers, and their individual capacity to grow and adapt.

Your goal

The overall goal of dealing with resistance to change is to gain your employees' intellectual and emotional acceptance of that change. This is known as "buy-in."

When employees buy in to a change initiative, they tend to respond positively to what's happening.

They feel a connection to the personal and organizational goals of the change, and develop an understanding of how change is beneficial to them and to the organization.

But employees won't automatically buy in to change. It will only happen if you have a relationship of trust and mutual confidence with them.

To develop trust and encourage your employees' buy-in to workplace change, you'll need to use three general techniques for dealing with resistance:
- open communication,
- employee involvement, and
- change agents.

TECHNIQUES FOR DEALING WITH RESISTERS

Techniques for dealing with resisters
Change can't happen without communication. This is because you can't create change without making decisions, you can't make decisions without information, and information has to be communicated. The first technique for dealing with resistance is to use open communication. This involves three main approaches.
provide information upfront
People are more likely to accept change when they understand it. To foster trust, you'll need to provide employees with information up front in the early stages of change. This way, resistance can be recognized and rectified before it becomes destructive. For example, you could provide information packages, or arrange question-and-answer sessions.
demonstrate transparency
Trust can only be accomplished by demonstrating transparency about the rationale behind the change and the effects it will have on the workforce. Managers who

tell employees "only what they need to know" foster a climate of resistance to change. They don't realize that fear of the unknown is often more threatening than even a harsh reality. If employees think you're hiding something, they'll jump to the conclusion it's something unpleasant.

communicate in person

One of the most difficult aspects of change is dealing with the variety and intensity of emotions your employees will experience. Written communication is an important part of obtaining employees' intellectual buy-in to change, but don't hide behind a flurry of e-mails, memos, and announcements. To obtain employees' emotional buy-in, it's best to communicate in person. Face-to-face interaction gives you immediate feedback on how your employees feel about the change, particularly through nonverbal behaviors – actions, facial expressions, and body language.

The second technique for dealing with resistance is to use employee involvement. As a manager, you're faced with the challenge of making sure employees buy in to the change. The best way to secure their commitment is to involve them in the process.

Communication is more than just broadcasting out. You'll never build trust with your employees without being able to listen to them as well. You can encourage two-way communication by asking for ideas, stimulating discussion, and listening to feedback.

By using their input, you'll give employees an active role in change and engage them in the process. The more engaged the employee, the higher their commitment to making change work.

Managing Organizational Change

Nora and August are both regional managers at a national information technology company. The company is undergoing change in the form of a transition from a hierarchical management structure to a team-based environment. Both managers realized the transition will mean employees will be taking on new responsibilities, accepting a new reporting structure, learning different ways of working together, and developing their interpersonal skills.

Follow along to find out how August coped with his region in the company's transition to a team-based business structure.

August relied on written communication. He compiled an information package for employees providing an outline of the new business structure, and his expectations for productivity.

Changes in work responsibilities and lines of authority were dealt with in e-mail memorandums to each of his managers on a need-to-know basis. Training in interpersonal skills was made mandatory for all employees.

The transition in August's region did not go smoothly because he neglected the emotional component of buy-in to change. Interpersonal conflicts disrupted many of his newly formed teams.

Resentful employees routinely missed training and those who did show up were skeptical that it would be of any use. Several junior managers left the company because they feared that the new structure would be detrimental to their career path.

Follow along to find out how Nora dealt with her region in the company's transition to a team-based business structure.

Nora relied on both written and face-to-face communication to communicate openly and involve her employees. Along with her information package, she held a series of meetings where upcoming changes were communicated to all the employees in her region.

Nora met face-to-face with each of her managers to discuss how the company's new lines of authority would function, and to get feedback about how they felt about the change. Training in interpersonal skills was arranged for employees who wanted it.

The transition in Nora's region went well because she provided information about the change up front, was transparent about what was happening, and obtained emotional buy-in by communicating in person with employees. She knew it was important to communicate feelings as well as facts.

By allowing employees input into the process, and a measure of control over the change, Nora was successful in dealing with resistance at the roots, before it became a major problem.

RECOGNIZING CHANGE AGENTS

Recognizing change agents
The third technique for dealing with resistance is to use change agents. Change agents are individuals who play a specific role in facilitating the change initiative. They don't necessarily have the direct authority to change things, but they do have the power to influence and motivate their fellow employees.

Change agents are valuable because their power base lies not with their authority, but with the respect and trust of their peers.

An important part of managing change is strategically choosing and persuading key players who can be brought on board as change agents.

Employees look to the change agent to model the new way of doing or thinking about things. If your change agent has an accepting attitude toward integrating change, it will influence overall participation and unity.

At the beginning of an initiative, it's not always apparent which employees are resistant to change. In fact, many of them will probably still be making up their minds. This group is where you're likely to find potential agents for change.

Change agents don't rush to intellectual judgment. They're respected by coworkers because their consideration of the facts makes their opinions credible.

Good change agents are also adept at understanding the emotional consequences of change. Search for an emotionally empathetic person, one who is sincerely concerned about how peers feel about what's happening.

Potential change agents are often those employees who display constructive resistance. Even though they're initially resistant to change, they'll usually be open to collaborating on mutually agreeable outcomes. If you listen, you'll pick up signals about what they need in order to accept and embrace change.

You're the general manager of a large financial services firm. Follow along as two potential change agents in your firm discuss their reaction to the firm's hiring of an IT company to implement a new information management system.

Renée: Look, I'm not opposed to the idea of improving the way we handle information, but our company is bringing in some IT firm that I've never heard of. I'm not confident outsiders understand the way things work around here.

Aaron: I have a bad feeling about this project. We haven't heard anything about how our departmental budgets will be affected. Change can be good, but at what cost? Will we have to lay people off if there's a shortfall?

To transform these resisters into change agents, you'll need to make them comfortable in the new environment and give them some control over the future. Renée needs

Managing Organizational Change

information about the methodology of the IT company before she can intellectually accept that the change is positive. Aaron needs to know how the project will affect department budgets to allay his fears about unknown cost impacts.

Question

You're a regional manager at a national computer company that is initiating a new business mentoring program. Based on the descriptions and statements of three resistant employees, who would you choose as a potential change agent for the project?

Options:

1. George
2. Mai
3. Zara

Answer

You'll need to review choosing a potential change agent.

Option 1: This option is incorrect. George isn't the best choice as a change agent. His avoidance of the issue shows passive resistance to the change. He doesn't offer any intellectual input as to what he needs or wants in order to accept the change. He gets along with his coworkers but doesn't show any particular empathy for how the change will affect them.

Option 2: This is the correct option. Mai is resistant, but her statements show she's open to accepting the change once her intellectual concerns are addressed. Her empathy for her coworkers' emotional concerns is also an important quality for a change agent.

Option 3: This option is incorrect. Even though she has the most work experience, Zara isn't the best choice as a change agent. She's actively resistant, and although she has authority with coworkers, her dictatorial approach doesn't demonstrate the empathy that would encourage coworkers to turn to her for emotional support.

Once you've recognized potential change agents, you'll need to provide opportunities to engage them in the initiative and help them develop a commitment to change.

HANDLING RESISTANCE WITH COMMUNICATION

Handling resistance with communication

Your employees can be powerful allies in implementing a successful change initiative. But first you'll need to deal with any issues that are creating resistance to the change. By using open communication and employee involvement, you can shape resistant employees into change agents.

Handling resistance to change involves using communication to create agents of change. To successfully gain Mai's buy-in to the change, you had to communicate openly with her by providing information up front and demonstrating transparency about what the change will involve. You also had to involve Mai in the change by using two-way communication to solicit and consider her input, and give her an active role in the change process.

CHAPTER 4 - SUSTAINING ORGANIZATIONAL CHANGE

CHAPTER 4 - Sustaining Organizational Change
   SECTION 1 - Creating a Collaborative Team Environment during Change
   SECTION 2 - Getting Employee Feedback Regarding Change
   SECTION 3 - Managing and Supporting Performance After Change

SECTION 1 - CREATING A COLLABORATIVE TEAM ENVIRONMENT DURING CHANGE

SECTION 1 - Creating a Collaborative Team Environment during Change

Change is unsettling for everyone, and it's likely that the relationships between you and your team members will come under some strain. Building rapport is a critical part of re-establishing a trusting and productive working environment. Team-building exercises build rapport, which in turn enhances collaboration.

But just like the change process itself, developing a collaborative team environment takes time. Be patient, and be prepared to deal with the insecurities and fears of team members. In the end, it'll be worth it, because when you encourage information sharing and foster shared ownership, team members pull together and ensure that the change process not only works but allows future improvements to flourish.

CREATE A COLLABORATIVE TEAM ENVIRONMENT

Create a collaborative team environment

As change comes and goes in your organization, relationships between individuals often come under stress. You and other managers spend time and effort pulling teams together, establishing good working relationships, and getting team members to truly rely on each other. Then, wham! Change happens, and everything can fall apart in an instant. Previous feelings of solidarity and team spirit can be taken over by anxieties, competitiveness, lack of trust, and feelings of isolation.

And it isn't just relationships that suffer when change occurs. When teams fall apart, productivity is reduced because the team isn't pulling together, and individual members may pursue personal agendas.

So how can you manage your team so the members support and maintain the benefits of change initiatives, instead of falling into conflict?

Managing Organizational Change

The first thing to do when a change process is coming to an end is to focus on supporting your team and enhancing rapport.

Almost everyone has met someone for the first time and felt an instant connection. That feeling – as though you'd known each other for years or have many of the same experiences – is rapport. It's a connected feeling of being on the same wavelength as someone else. When you have that affinity with someone, you can appreciate each other's feelings and understand the other person's viewpoint. Rapport leads to a harmonious and sympathetic relationship of mutual trust.

It's easy to understand how the ability to develop rapport is key to influencing others and can lead to being a persuasive speaker or a tremendous salesperson.

But developing rapport in the workplace can do more than that. It can open the way to creating a positive work environment where teamwork grows. And having team rapport is especially important when you're trying to maintain the momentum of a change initiative.

Better connectivity and communication build stronger, more effective teams that are able to do what it takes to sustain organizational change. But how can you strengthen these aspects in your team? Team-building exercises can be a useful tool for building this kind of rapport among team members.

Whatever team-building exercises you've been part of probably fell into one of three general categories. Some exercises promote fun and camaraderie, because teams work better if their members know each other well. Others are experiential learning exercises. These are especially important following change, because team members who lack experience with new systems or processes can feel isolated. And performance improvement exercises provide team members with knowledge they need to do their jobs better.

Fun and camaraderie exercises

Fun and camaraderie building exercises give team members the chance to interact in nonwork situations.

Social outings, sporting activities, or collective tasks such as drama groups allow team members to get to know each other in relaxed circumstances. Barbecues, scavenger hunts, softball leagues, and charity work are all ways to break down barriers.

Experiential learning exercises

Experiential learning exercises give employees the chance to role-play or practice dealing with work situations in safe circumstances.

You can run workshops where you let employees play the roles of customers or managers, or get them to consider production or safety issues and how they might react. Getting everyone involved means nobody worries about making mistakes.

Performance improvement exercises

After change, it takes time for employees to learn new practices. Performance improvement exercises may involve coaching, sharing best practices, or discussing hints and tips.

Consider getting sales team members to attend a sales closing course, hiring a customer service expert to talk to customer service representatives, or holding a best practices seminar. Performance improvement exercises aim to help employees to become confident with new systems and procedures.

Fun and camaraderie building exercises are especially useful when the team has new members, or if there's been conflict during the change. But be sure you take team members' personal circumstances into account. For instance, don't arrange a lot of after-hours activities if employees have families or travel long distances.

Experiential learning exercises are great when there's been significant change in procedures. They're useful when employees have to deal with – or are reluctant to adopt – a new system or procedure. But if the change doesn't impact processes, these exercises aren't appropriate.

Performance improvement exercises can bring team members up to previous levels of productivity, or help them meet challenging targets. Don't use them if the changes are only structural, because experienced team members may feel patronized.

Building rapport and cohesion on a team can bring many benefits to an organization, enabling it to better sustain changes. Team building reinvigorates interdepartmental and companywide idea sharing, which helps ensure that changes are solidified throughout the company. By encouraging employee interaction through games, tasks, and activities, you can more easily get everyone on the same page in relation to the new systems and processes.

Question

A team has just undergone a major change initiative, and things are finally starting to settle down.

Based on what you've learned about rapport, what do you think the benefits would be to this team if it built rapport through team-building exercises?

Options:
1. The team will have better communication
2. The team will have increased effectiveness in achieving goals
3. The team will collaborate better
4. The team will be more creative and innovative
5. The organization will have a greater return on investment
6. The team will be able to return to previous ways of working

Answer

Option 1: This is a correct option. When people develop rapport, better communication results. By getting everyone to work with one another on team-building exercises, you improve active listening and observation skills. This helps eliminate preconceptions and miscommunications.

Option 2: This is a correct option. Increased effectiveness in achieving goals is a result of rapport and team building. Members feel more confident and inspired to tackle their own targets, as well as the company's. Increased production, creative output, and ingenuity are all benefits of team-building exercises.

Option 3: This is a correct option. Team-building exercises help members trust each other. Collaboration flourishes in such an environment of loyalty.

Option 4: This is a correct option. When a team is working well, team members collaborate effectively and communicate freely. When everyone pulls together, ideas are generated, innovation comes to the fore, and creativity can flourish.

Option 5: This is an incorrect option. While better teamwork can result in higher productivity, and sometimes enhanced ROI, team-building exercises aren't specifically designed to increase ROI.

Option 6: This is an incorrect option. Change has happened, so team members will never be able to return to their previous ways of working. They need to focus on the future and working together.

Teams that use team-building exercises to increase rapport after change will reap many benefits, such as better communication and collaboration, and enhanced innovation and effectiveness. But keep in mind that team building should be done before and during change initiatives, not just after. It should be ongoing; it shouldn't be based on "getting back to normal" after change. The old normality is based on old ways of working, and those are gone.

FOSTER COLLABORATION AFTER CHANGE

Foster collaboration after change

Since there's no going back, new processes and practices have to be learned, so a collaborative team environment is vital. By encouraging teamwork, you'll ensure your changes are incorporated and that you can build toward future change and improvement. Collaboration enables a team to achieve results no individual could produce alone. If you can encourage collaboration among your team members, you can ensure the results of the change process are extraordinary and long-standing.

But what is collaboration, really? Simply put, collaboration is the heart of good teamwork. It's a method of working together in an atmosphere of trust and support. Collaboration begins with seeking common ground – that is, establishing rapport. Collaboration is based on good communication.

What truly distinguishes collaboration from other ways of working is that it's a mutually beneficial and well-defined relationship. When you collaborate, your goal isn't just a specified target or output. Of course you have to achieve your desired deliverable or outcome, but you want to do it in the most efficient and effective way possible. Collaboration allows you to do that. So you need to pay just as much attention to how you work together as you do to the work itself.

Characteristics of collaborative team members

Because true collaboration requires a culture of sharing, truly collaborative teams share responsibility, resources, and credit for achieving mutual goals. Team members trust each other, never blaming, ambushing, or surprising each other. They help each other succeed, and they achieve more together than they could individually.

As a manager or leader, you can cultivate collaboration among team members. But collaborative working requires each team member to relinquish individual control to the team as a whole. The idea of "working jointly" is crucial to collaboration. It's also a critical part of ensuring that changes become effectively integrated into your organization's ways of working.

But collaboration can be a challenge with employees who think of themselves as individual "stars." To overcome challenges to promoting collaboration, your goal as a leader is to promote a culture of sharing among your employees. In such a culture, individual employees perceive themselves as part of a greater whole. To achieve this collaborative culture, you can apply two simple techniques: fostering shared ownership among your team members and encouraging information sharing.

Select each collaboration technique for more information and examples of how you can apply the technique on your team.

Foster shared ownership

To foster shared ownership, whenever possible, try to allocate shared responsibilities. Actively encourage individuals to relinquish individual control of projects or tasks.

At its simplest, you foster shared ownership by giving two or more people shared responsibility for a project. At a higher level, you can set up self-managed cross-functional teams, where the whole team has responsibility for setting objectives and managing personnel issues.

Encourage information sharing

Encouraging information sharing isn't simply making sure that everyone knows what's happening. To promote collaboration, encourage team members to share best practices, talk openly about problems that have arisen, and discuss ideas freely.

Share information through methods such as formal meetings, knowledge-sharing databases, and "best practice-sharing" e-mails. Publicly praise those who share information.

Question

You work for a large oil company, and you've taken responsibility for the company's new customer service policy. The policy was implemented a few weeks ago, and now you need to incorporate the change by creating a collaborative team environment.

Match each strategy for promoting collaboration with one or more corresponding examples. You may use each strategy more than once.

Options:
A. Encouraging information sharing
B. Fostering shared ownership

Targets:
1. Ask team members to describe how they've overcome customer complaints
2. Give two team members joint responsibility for creating a customer survey
3. Hold a meeting to let employees discuss best practices in customer service
4. Ask an employee working on an extensive project where others may help out

Answer

Encouraging information sharing includes getting employees to talk about their past experiences to improve practices in the future.

A great way to foster shared ownership is to divide responsibility for certain tasks between two or more coworkers. Employees will feel equally responsible for the team's or organization's success.

You can encourage information sharing by getting employees together to discuss best practices, experiences, or knowledge.

Fostering shared ownership often means ensuring that all employees are involved in projects or they're able to contribute to interesting or exciting activities.

Sometimes collaborating can be difficult. As a leader, you may encounter situations when you'd prefer to take on additional responsibilities rather than delegate. Or maybe you feel it's more efficient to tell employees how to do things instead of listening to ideas. However, you need your employees to buy in to changes and feel they have some say in what the future looks like. Collaboration is the only way they will truly adapt to the change and continue to develop.

Foster shared ownership

When you're trying to foster shared ownership, remember that employees may not want to give up control of tasks. You have to be sensitive and avoid behaving in a dictatorial or mistrustful way. Be sympathetic to concerns and don't imply that loss of sole ownership is a punishment.

For example, you might say "Working together will help the team be more cross-functional and independent, which in turn will raise everyone's visibility within the organization." Don't say anything like "This is the new way of working, and you'll just have to get used to it."

Encourage information sharing

When encouraging information sharing, simply asking employees to share information isn't enough. You may have to draw information from reluctant individuals, such as with a statement like "I hear what you're saying, and you make a good point."

Just because you're the leader doesn't mean that you're the only one who can be right. Be sure you don't make comments like "You may not like it, but it's my decision." That kind of talk won't get employees to open up and share information.

The new project is complex and requires your team members to work closely together. This is a real opportunity to incorporate recent changes. Although everyone has individual goals and responsibilities, on a truly collaborative team, the goals of the team should always be the main focus. Promoting shared ownership of those goals is how a group of people becomes a true team.

SECTION 2 - GETTING EMPLOYEE FEEDBACK REGARDING CHANGE

SECTION 2 - Getting Employee Feedback Regarding Change

However successful the process of change has been, there's always room for improvement.

By including your employees in reviewing processes and systems, you can help individuals develop and improve their own performances. You can also encourage openness and honesty across the organization, and show others that you and your employees are striving to achieve more.

Suggestion boxes, questionnaires, focus groups, and one-on-one discussions are all useful methods for collecting feedback from your employees.

COLLECTING EMPLOYEE FEEDBACK

Collecting employee feedback

SECTION 3 - MANAGING AND SUPPORTING PERFORMANCE AFTER CHANGE

SECTION 3 - Managing and Supporting Performance After Change

Performance management is often put aside during the chaotic times of change implementation. But if your change is going to stick, you need to reintroduce performance management strategies and mechanisms as quickly as possible.

Managing and supporting performance after change involves providing ongoing training and development and rewarding continued improvement. Sustaining performance also depends on establishing and maintaining effective performance standards and providing feedback.

Feedback is key to maintaining performance standards. If you apply the three feedback steps – identifying the performance issue, evaluating the performance, and developing a solution – you'll help ensure your feedback is well received and performance improves.

MANAGING PERFORMANCE AFTER CHANGE

Managing performance after change

It's easy to forget that change isn't an end to improvement – it's a beginning. During the change process, people work hard to get the change initiative implemented and tend to worry about details later. But once the change is over, how are you going to get a hold of the details then? And how will you use them to ensure that high levels of performance are reached and maintained? Managing performance is always important but, after a change, it's critical.

Taking the initiative to manage performance after a change can bring significant benefits:
- it will ensure productivity by dealing with performance problems quickly and effectively,
- it will support the ongoing development of employees and ensure their effective transition,
- it will give employees a clear idea of what's expected and build the confidence they need to sustain change, and

- it will help you avoid the conflicts and inefficiencies that inevitably arise when poor performance is left unchecked.

Performance management often takes second place during the chaotic times of change implementation. But if your change is going to stick, you need to reintroduce performance management strategies and mechanisms as quickly as possible. To manage and support performance after change, you need to provide ongoing training and development, reward ongoing improvement, maintain effective performance standards, and provide feedback on performance.

Improvements can be generated as the result of good ideas and hard work, but individuals also need training if they're going to sustain ongoing improvements.

Training can help your employees develop new skills, expand their existing knowledge, and explore new ideas. It can also benefit you as a manager by boosting morale and making employees feel valued.

When considering how to implement training and development, you can use several strategies. Coaching, formal seminars or workshops, discovery training, job rotation, and programmed learning are all handy tactics to develop the skills of your employees and to help ensure changes are maintained.

Coaching

Coaching involves supporting employees on a one-on-one basis to help them improve their skills and knowledge in a particular job area. Coaching is an ongoing interaction that includes questions, answers, demonstrations, and experiments, so be prepared to invest the necessary time and effort.

Formal seminars or workshops

Formal seminars or workshops are usually one-time events that focus on helping employees gain the skills or knowledge to deal with a single issue, such as a new procedure or recent development. They're highly structured events that may include some handouts and some hands-on practice, but they don't provide ongoing support.

Job rotation

Job rotation focuses on getting employees to better understand job roles and requirements. But in job rotation, employees regularly swap jobs with each other to gain insight into what's expected of colleagues. This encourages empathy and a better understanding of how the other parts of the company operate while revealing areas of overlap and conflict.

Programmed learning

Programmed learning allows employees to progress at their own speeds using workbooks, textbooks, e-learning materials, seminars, or other resources. Information is presented with periodic assessments to test learning and provide feedback to employees as they progress. Programmed learning offers employees the opportunity for long-term development and can be customized to a particular situation.

Opportunities for training and development can be made all the more effective if people are given incentives to make use of them. Recognition and rewards can drive acceptance of change. People are, by nature, reluctant to move toward the unknown. Rewards for ongoing learning and improvement can motivate people to learn new skills specific to the change.

Becoming more proficient in the new ways of doing things will speed up acceptance of change. A pay system or a bonus system based on skill development is particularly appropriate if the organizational change involves a commitment to continued improvement.

Rewards can take a variety of forms under two broad categories:

Monetary incentives can be in the form of tuition reimbursements, bonuses, paid educational leaves, or time set aside at work for continuing education and personal or professional development.

Nonmonetary incentives might include offering employees the chance to job shadow someone in a role they aspire to. Or it could involve basic recognition of efforts, such as an employee of the month program or other periodic award.

Following change, it's important that you put in place standards to establish the new levels of performance you expect from your employees. The cornerstone of sustaining ongoing improvement is to maintain effective performance standards, ensuring employees can meet those requirements by giving them effective feedback.

Providing effective feedback on performance helps employees meet the standards and continue to improve. Giving feedback is a valuable way of ensuring that issues about performance are brought out into the open.

Question

Which activities are necessary for managing and supporting performance after change?

Options:

1. Providing ongoing training and development
2. Rewarding ongoing improvement

3. Maintaining effective performance standards
4. Providing feedback on performance
5. Getting executive buy-in
6. Ensuring cultural change through charismatic leadership

Answer

Option 1: This is a correct option. You provide ongoing training and development so that individuals can achieve their potential and sustain ongoing improvements.

Option 2: This is a correct option. You reward ongoing improvement to motivate employees to take advantage of the opportunities you've provided for training and development.

Option 3: This is a correct option. Establishing and maintaining effective performance standards lets employees know what's expected of them regarding maintaining the change.

Option 4: This is a correct option. Providing feedback gives employees the information they need to meet standards and brings performance issues out in the open.

Option 5: This is an incorrect option. While executive buy-in may be needed to implement changes to incentive and reward systems, it's not a specific method for performance management.

Option 6: This is an incorrect option. Charismatic leadership won't help employees with the nitty-gritty of their jobs the way training, rewards, feedback, and standards will.

MAINTAINING PERFORMANCE STANDARDS

Maintaining performance standards

Supporting ongoing performance improvement with training and rewards must be tied to clear and effective standards that establish the levels of performance you expect from your employees. Standards should be developed with care, otherwise they may end up irrelevant or inappropriately focused. If they're well thought out and effective, performance standards will have certain characteristics: they'll be job-specific, clearly connected with organizational goals, and based on measurable outcomes.

Job-specific

Performance-related standards must be defined and measurable. They need to be specific to the job and not dependent on other jobs, which allows for comparison between employees. You should be able to measure how effectively the task has been performed and be able to compare performances between individuals doing the same task.

For example, if you're a customer service manager, a standard requiring your call handlers to "provide 100% of callers with the information they request, or redirect them to the appropriate department" is specific to the job that call handlers are responsible for. "Ensure that callers are happy with the information they receive from this center" is not. The standard isn't specific to a given job but relies on a number of different departments to perform various jobs successfully.

Clearly connected with organizational goals

Standards should be tied to organizational goals so they add value to the organization and its workforce.

If an organization has a goal of "providing the most innovative products in the field," a standard requiring R&D to "reduce research costs by 20%" isn't linked to the greater organizational goal. It would be more appropriate in this case to set a standard to "increase the number of new products to market by 20%."

Based on measurable outcomes

Standards should be based on measurable outcomes, not activities. Activities are the actions that produce the outcomes, which are the outputs.

"Filing documents" is an activity, whereas "100% of files being orderly and complete" is an outcome. It's an output with qualitative or quantitative measurements.

A standard of "zero goods returned" is a suitable standard for an organization's quality improvement initiative, whereas a standard of "check the first and last sample from every batch" is not, as it's related to simply completing an activity.

For example, consider the call center where Verner is a manager. It's undergone a massive reorganization following a recent acquisition. Verner is developing new criteria to monitor and improve performance.

Verner needs to set a performance standard for the team members who answer calls and transfer them to the relevant departments. As a whole, the organization aims to "offer exceptional standards of customer service."

Verner is experienced and knows standards should be specific and measurable, connected with organizational goals, and outcome-based. His performance standard states "All calls will be answered within three rings, and transferred to an appropriate person in less than one minute."

Job-specific

The performance standard refers specifically to the tasks performed by call handlers. It allows clear comparisons between the performance of different individuals doing the same task.

Clearly connected with organizational goals

Verner's performance standard clearly builds toward the overall organizational goal to "offer exceptional standards of customer service." This goal will be met if calls are answered within three rings and handled effectively within one minute.

Based on measurable outcomes

The standard refers to the accomplishment of the call reaching the appropriate person within one minute. Verner can measure this output easily by making a quantitative measurement of how long it takes to transfer the call and who receives it.

Meeting the criteria for effective standards

The standard is specific to the job of a laboratory technician, since it covers all the basic duties. However,

Managing Organizational Change

it's not clearly connected with the organization's goals, as it doesn't emphasize accuracy or adherence to regulations.

The standard also lacks measurable outcomes, as the duties are vague and not defined with metrics. If it said, for example, that all glassware should be sterilized within four hours of use, that outcome could be measured. The standard of "keep neat and easily interpreted records" also isn't measurable.

Question

Rico is the manager of a sales team. He's been researching creating performance standards for his sales representatives. As the organization has a new goal of retaining more customers, Rico set a standard to "ensure that individual sales are improved each month by talking regularly to customers."

Which statement correctly describes the characteristics of this performance standard?

Options:

1. It's not job-specific, based on measurable outcomes, or connected to organizational goals

2. It's based on measurable outcomes

3. It's connected to organizational goals

4. It's specific and organization focused, but it isn't based on measurable accomplishments

5. It exhibits all the characteristics of an effective performance standard

6. It's job-specific and based on measurable accomplishments but not connected to organizational goals

Answer

In fact, Rico's performance standard doesn't meet the three criteria because it relates to people instead of tasks, relates to activities and not outputs, and doesn't clearly fit into the organizational goal to provide excellent customer service.

Option 1: This is the correct option. Rico's standard isn't specific to the job, based on measurable outcomes, or connected to organizational goals. It doesn't approach the job in a way that will allow comparisons, isn't possible to measure, and is aligned to a sales goal, not the organizational goal of retaining more customers.

Option 2: This option is incorrect. Rico's standard focuses on the activity of talking and not on a measurable accomplishment or output, such as the number of sales.

Option 3: This option is incorrect. Rico's standard isn't specifically aligned with the organizational goal of retaining more customers but rather to a sales goal.

Option 4: This option is incorrect. The standard is too specific to individuals to be job-specific and doesn't relate to the organizational goal of retaining more customers.

Option 5: This option is incorrect. None of the three criteria are satisfied by this standard. It's not directed at the organizational goal, it doesn't target specific outcomes, and it addresses individual performance, rather than focusing on the job.

Option 6: This option is incorrect. The standard is too specific to individuals to be job-specific and isn't focused on a measurable accomplishment such as the number of repeat customers.

PROVIDING FEEDBACK ON PERFORMANCE

Providing feedback on performance

No matter how great your performance standards are, it's not enough to just create them. You also have to monitor performance to ensure those standards are being met. And you must give employees the feedback they need to proceed confidently and adjust their performance if necessary to sustain the change. Giving feedback to your employees also helps ensure performance issues are brought out into the open. But giving feedback – particularly negative feedback – can be tricky.

So how can you give feedback effectively? Different types of feedback strategies are available to you:
- performance reviews, which are regular meetings to review an employee's performance against goals and to improve future performance, and
- informal check-up sessions, which should be used frequently with all employees to give praise, guidance, and support.

Both of these feedback methods require that you focus on particular measures of performance, as outlined by the established performance standards.

Performance reviews

Performance reviews usually include examining employee strengths and weaknesses to improve effectiveness and efficiency. These meetings may help to determine why a person is failing to achieve targets and can be used to agree on remedial actions. They may also identify someone's secret to success, allowing you to share best practices.

Informal praise and check-up sessions

Check-up sessions and the informal giving of praise should be used frequently after major change to congratulate employees on good performance, evaluate their situations, and ask whether they need any additional support or guidance.

Informal praise and check-ups should occur whenever you recognize the need, on a spontaneous basis. But a more formal situation such as a performance review should use a more standardized approach to giving feedback. This type of feedback process has three steps: identify the performance issue, evaluate performance, and develop a solution.

Step 1 – Identify the performance issue

As a first step in giving feedback to an individual, you have to identify the performance issue to discuss. Although some performance reviews will be overwhelmingly positive, most will address one or more issues that call for some kind of improvement. Usually, the issue will be some area where performance is weak, as indicated by errors, missed deadlines, mistakes, or other incidents that bring the performance issue to your attention.

Make sure you've noticed the performance issue yourself, and talk only about the facts of the situation. Don't make assumptions about how the employee is feeling, don't act on rumor, and don't hint around about the issue – be direct.

Step 2 – Evaluate performance

When you've determined what issue you're going to give feedback on, you need to evaluate performance. The best way to do this is to compare the employee's performance against agreed-upon criteria such as standards, targets, performance indicators, procedures, or measures of accuracy.

When you evaluate your employee's performance, be fair. Use clearly defined criteria and avoid passing personal judgments. Link your comments to facts, and don't express disappointment or anger when you speak to your employee.

Step 3 – Develop a solution

Finally, make sure you work with your employee to develop a solution to the issue that you've identified. Typical solutions might include additional training or coaching, or rethinking deadlines or ways of working. You might also need to adjust schedules and deadlines or change procedures.

Don't give feedback to employees without being prepared to work with them to develop solutions. If resources or additional support are required, make them available. You shouldn't expect employees to solve problems on their own.

Consider Xavier, the manager of a building supply store. One of his employees, Tamiko, needs feedback about mistakes on some invoices. She's occasionally failed to take into account customer discounts and special offers when charging customers. After a recent database overhaul, employees are now supposed to enter a customer account code to determine whether any discounts apply. Tamiko isn't using the updated procedures, so Xavier meets with her to give her feedback.

Follow along as Xavier meets with Tamiko to talk to her about her performance.

Xavier: Tamiko, in going over some of your recent invoices, I found one area where you've been making a mistake. Customers have been getting charged inconsistently because you're not using the new customer code procedure.

Tamiko: I guess I needed to check the discounts and offers against the new sales database. I'm really embarrassed about the mistakes I've made with the invoices. I just can't seem to get used to the new software.

Xavier: Well, if you had used the customer code procedure correctly, I'd never have noticed. Maybe it's for the best, because it seems customer codes aren't the entire problem here. The new system is confusing you overall.

Tamiko: Yes it is. The real problem is that I don't understand how to make use of all the new functions, so I've only been using the functions I do understand.

Xavier: Why don't you work alongside Wendy for a while so she can teach you how to use it properly?

Managing Organizational Change

Tamiko: That's a great idea, thanks. I'm sure it won't take long to get used to things if I can shadow her for a short while.

Xavier covered each of the three steps in his conversation with Tamiko. In step 1, he identified the performance issue of customers being charged inconsistently. In step 2, Xavier evaluated Tamiko's performance using the clear measurement of using or not using the new customer code procedure.

In step 3, he worked with Tamiko to understand the underlying problem, which is a lack of overall comfort with the new system. Then they developed a solution to the problem by having Tamiko job shadow a more experienced employee.

Question

You've just introduced changes to the way your employees manage client accounts, and you're using individual performance feedback to help sustain the change. Alonso is one of your team members.

Sequence the actions that you take to give performance feedback to Alonso by matching the steps to actions that would take place in each step. You may use each step more than once.

Options:
A. Step 1
B. Step 2
C. Step 3

Targets:

1. You tell Alonso he hasn't processed as many customer orders this month as he should

2. You point out how Alonso's metrics aren't reaching the new performance target

3. You arrange for Alonso to attend a half-day training course to teach him how to use the ordering system

4. You check your records and find Alonso is processing significantly fewer orders than you expected

5. You show Alonso his performance data and relate it to the team's average

REFERENCES

References
- **Implementing Electronic Document and Record Management Systems** - 2008, Adam Azad, Auerbach Publications
- **Built to Change: How to Achieve Sustained Organizational Effectiveness** - 2006, Edward E. Lawler III and Christopher G. Worley, Jossey-Bass
- **Enterprise-Wide Change: Superior Results Through Systems Thinking** - 2005, Stephen G. Haines, Gail Aller-Stead, and James McKinlay, Pfeiffer
- **Sustainable Business Development: Inventing the Future Through Strategy, Innovation, and Leadership** -2006, David L. Rainey, Cambridge University Press

GLOSSARY

Glossary
A
active resistance - Open and overt resistive behavior. See also passive resistance.

authoritarian - A person in authority who exercises complete or near complete control over the actions of subordinates.

authority - The power or right to give orders and instructions and to make decisions.

B
benign neglect -Appearing to agree with a change but intentionally not following through with any support.

C
change - 1. A transformation, modification, variation, or alteration of the norm. 2. The passing from one state, phase, form, or culture to another.

coaching - Supporting employees on a one-on-one basis to help them gain the skills or knowledge they need to fulfill their job roles.

coercive power - A type of power based on fear used by those in a position to intimidate or punish employees.

common vision - An influencing style that involves identifying and articulating what the future could be, and appealing to the hopes, values, and aspirations of employees to help them believe that outcomes can be achieved through their efforts.

constructive resistance - Resistance motivated by an individual's desire to collaborate on a change solution that protects the best interests of the organization.

D

discovery training - A task that involves employees reviewing their jobs in detail, giving consideration to the purpose of their job, how it's done, and whether it could be done differently, leading to an end result of developing both their roles and their skills.

E

empirical-rational approach - An approach to change built on the assumption that people are basically reasonable and they will do what they think is good for them. Users of this approach try to get buy-in by convincing stakeholders of the need for change through communication, persuasion, and incentives.

environmental-adaptive approach - An approach to change built on the assumption that people adjust quickly to change. With large changes, it may be easier to make the change and place the burden on individuals to adapt.

evolutionary change - One of the two broad categories of organizational change along with transformational change. Evolutionary change, which can take the form of strategic adjustments or strategic reorientation, is incremental change that occurs over time.

F

focus group - Also called open forum, this group considers a range of opinions on a specific topic and then produces very focused feedback quickly.

force field analysis - Proposed by Kurt Lewin, a method of weighing the pros and cons of a change.

I

initiative - An organizational program, project, or effort that has a specific purpose, goals, and objectives.

J

job rotation - A process of employees swapping jobs to gain a better understanding of how the company operates, recognize areas of overlap and conflict, and get an appreciation of how their actions impact on others within the organization and on customers.

M

malicious compliance - A form of malicious resistance where rules or procedures are deliberately followed to the letter in an attempt to sabotage productivity, rather than to serve their purpose. Also known as letter-of-the-law compliance.

N

normative - reeducative approach - An approach to change built on the assumption that, because humans are social animals, the primary factor influencing people's behavior is a desire to conform to group values and norms. This type of approach is socially and culturally focused.

O

one-on-one discussion - Speaking directly to employees to find out exactly what's happening on the team and to elicit detailed feedback about specific issues. When using this method, it's important to focus on the systems, not on the individual.

P

passive resistance - Undisclosed and covert resistive behavior. See also active resistance.

power-coercive approach - An approach to change built on the assumption that people expect those in charge to tell them what to do and will be inclined to simply do what they're told. Employees are expected to comply or face sanctions.

praise and check-up sessions - Regular, informal sessions that involve a manager offering praise, guidance, and support as necessary. They're very effective at maintaining motivation.

programmed learning - Instruction that allows employees to progress at their own speed using workbooks, textbooks, e-learning materials, seminars, or other resources. Information is presented in distinct elements and each element involves assessment both to test learning and to provide immediate feedback to the employee about achievement.

Q

questionnaire - A document containing several questions that allow users to choose answers from a series of options, or write individual responses. It can be anonymous or attributed to an employee, and provides structured feedback on specific issues.

R

rallying - Mobilizing people to support a common purpose.

resistance - Non-compliant behavior.

resister - An individual who deliberately obstructs change.

S

short-term win - A goal based on clearly stated, measurable, and easily identifiable criteria. The results must be conclusive, straightforward to interpret, and impossible to misinterpret.

suggestion box - A system that allows employees to put forward ideas about how systems or practices could improve. The box can be physical or operated via a web site, and feedback can be submitted on a form or in a format chosen by the employee. The feedback received can be random. Feedback is anonymous.

T

transformational change - One of the two broad categories of organizational change along with evolutionary change. Transformational change involves a fundamental re-evaluation and redirection of an organization's core business.

transition - The process and reaction that an individual goes through when dealing with a change in situation, process, or circumstances. The three stage are end, neutral zone (or middle), and beginning.

transparency - Actions and communication free from pretence or deceit.

www.ingramcontent.com/pod-product-compliance
Lightning Source LLC
Chambersburg PA
CBHW020913180526
45163CB00007B/2716